LESSON PLANS

Writing
for a
Global
Perspective

Pat Nickell ▪ Liz Barrett

a publication of
National Council for the Social Studies

KENDALL/HUNT PUBLISHING COMPANY
2460 Kerper Boulevard P.O. Box 539 Dubuque, Iowa 52004-0539

Editorial Staff on this publication:

Salvatore Natoli, Director of Publications, NCSS

Layout and design: Dan Kaufman, Coordinator of Desktop Publishing, NCSS

Copyright © 1991 by National Council for the Social Studies

Library of Congress Catalog Card Number: 90-64473

ISBN 0-8403-6502-0

Printed in the United States of America
10 9 8 7 6 5 4 3 2 1

Table of Contents

About the Authors

Pat Nickell is Coordinator of Social Studies and Bluegrass International Program for the Fayette County Schools, Lexington, Kentucky. She is on the NCSS Board of Directors where she serves as Vice Chair of the Middle School Task Force, and she has held membership on the International Activities Advisory Committee.

Liz Barrett is a seventh grade teacher of social studies at Tates Creek Middle School, Lexington, Kentucky. She is on the Steering Committee of Bluegrass International Program and serves as the middle school representative to the Steering Committee of the Fayette County Council for the Social Studies.

Acknowledgements

The authors wish to recognize the Longview Foundation for their generous funding of this project and their longstanding support of global education. We also wish to thank Dr. Angene Wilson for her leadership and encouragement for the project. Finally we appreciate Marlene Watkins's tremendous effort and immense patience.

Preface

This handbook is created for use by Social Studies and English teachers at the middle school level. Activities will generate interest in global issues while providing experience and direction in writing. The handbook presents war, hunger, human rights, deforestation, and other problems threatening our world in interesting and highly personal ways that will spark the global concern and altruistic spirit students at this age have, but rarely ponder or act upon.

Recent advances in the approaches to teaching writing, including the realization that students *learn* from the writing process, point out the value of combining writing instruction with various other subjects within the curriculum.

Additionally, "central to the idea of using writing to learn is the understanding that learning is promoted this way only if the writing is perceived as purposeful *by the writer*" (Mayher, Lester, and Pradl. *Learning to Write/Writing to Learn*, 1983). Both using writing to learn about the world and providing students meaningful purposes for writing are incorporated as goals of this handbook.

Teachers may use the lessons as individual units or scatter them over a semester or school year. Teachers may present the lessons in any order with the exception of Lesson #8, which summarizes and culminates the teachings of the others.

"...we, quite literally, are potentially defenseless on this earth unless global, as well as domestic, problems are handled in a way that fuses aspirations for peace and security with the inevitability of change."
—Report of the Study Commission on Global Education, 1988

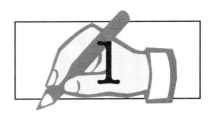

Writing Skill:	**Writing a Fable**
Global Issue:	**War**
World Region:	**Northern Ireland**
Class Periods Required:	**2**

Rationale:

Although story-writing is a common task assigned to young students, it often results in a rather disjointed series of weakly developed events, frequently devoid of theme, plot, well-defined setting, or character development. If we provided student's samples, a theme to work from, and the knowledge that the story can be brief, yet meaningful, results will improve and students will gain understanding of the importance of structure.

The conflict in Northern Ireland provides an unlikely setting for a real-life fable recently described in the *Denver Post.* The struggle between Catholics and Protestants takes on immediacy as students read about something that will touch their hearts—a little dog named Scruffy.

Objectives:

1. Students will gain information about the conflict in Northern Ireland.
2. Students will be able to define a fable.
3. Given a theme (moral) students will write a fable.

Materials Needed:

1. Copy of Handout #1.
2. One copy per student of the news article "Catholics, Protestants Loved Scruffy the Dog—and He's Gone" (Handout #2)
3. Optional: Newspaper or news magazine articles dealing with the conflict in Northern Ireland. (Provided by teacher)
4. Optional: A copy of *Aesop's Fables* (Provided by teacher)

Background Information:

Northern Ireland remains under British Rule although its southern neighbor, the Irish Republic, gained independence in 1921 whereas Northern Ireland is predominantly Protestant, minority Catholics would prefer to unite with the Irish Republic. Local Protestant leaders are accused of discriminating against the Catholics in political and social matters. Protestants, preferring to maintain ties with London, turned over their control to Parliament in the early 1970s, hoping strong leadership from Britain's capital would end the strife. Even the British armed forces have been unable to quell the violence of the Irish Republican Army (IRA) and terrorist subgroups.

Instructional Strategies:

Day 1

1. Ask for about 7 to 9 volunteers to participate in a role-play. Distribute copies of Handout. Allow a few minutes for them to read over the scenario and discuss plans for performing it before the class. Once they have acted out the scenario for the other students, ask them what phenomenon or significant characteristic in human nature was illustrated by the role-play. Discuss.

2. Then ask students to share whatever knowledge they have about the conflict in Northern Ireland. If desired, allow volunteers to gather additional information from news articles, etc., to present to the class on ensuing days. Have students locate Northern Ireland on a map, noting its close proximity to England and Western Europe. Be certain students understand that Northern Ireland is a developed, industrialized nation and part of the United Kingdom.

3. Distribute copies of the news article (Handout #2) and explain to students that the article describes a side of Northern Ireland's conflict that, although heart-warming, should be taken in the context of a bitter, bloody civil war.

4. Have students read the article silently or select a strong reader to read aloud as others follow along.

5. Have students underline portions of the article dealing specifically with the war, then reread just those portions. By doing so, students are helped to recognize the grim setting in which the lighter story occurs and it thus becomes all the more poignant.

6. Now have students restate the Scruffy story itself and discuss the effects the dog has had on various events in the civil conflict.

7. Ask students to discuss that aspect of human nature the story illustrates (i.e., even when people staunchly support one side of an issue against another, both sides can unite to achieve a common goal. Further, once they achieved that goal, either side may again be reestablished and resume conflict).

8. Have students attempt to construct a "moral" that would apply to both the earlier role-play and the news article. The teacher should write the finished product on the chalkboard for all students to copy.

9. Ask students what characterizes a story that has a moral. Guide them as needed to conclude that fables require a moral. Their purpose is to teach a lesson about human behavior. They may also correctly characterize fables as often featuring animals as the characters.

10. You may wish to read several of *Aesop's Fables* or have student volunteers do so.

11. For class the next day, assign students to write a fable, using the moral they constructed as their theme.

Day 2

1. Have students share their fables in small groups or before the class.

Follow-up

As additional current events lessons bring global issues into focus, students may be interested in developing themes, morals, character studies, and other story starters. Fables, poetry, song lyrics, role-plays, and other forms of expression will serve as effective outlets for feelings students may have about issues with which they feel powerless to deal.

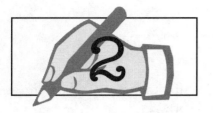

Writing Skill:	**Writing Reader-Based Prose**
Global Issue:	**Illegal Narcotics Trafficking**
World Region:	**Worldwide**
Class Periods Required:	**2-3**

Rationale:

Crime in the United States is a major issue that consumes much of the government's energy and assets. Large urban areas suffer the most; local governments are forced to withstand an enormous drain on human and financial resources.

The illegal drug economy in the United States is at the forefront of the crime dilemma. Its changing complexity and sophistication make illegal drug sales a baffling puzzle even for experts in crime prevention. A primary complication is that most of the substances filter into the United States from countries whose governments are incapable of stemming the outward flow from within.

As with most national issues, a vast array of statistics and information are available on the drug problem. We must be able to process this avalanche of information through the print and visual media. This exercise provides practice in transforming a technical piece of information into a written summary that will have use and meaning for the student. This creation of "reader-based prose" gives students practice in writing without assuming their audience is as informed or more informed than they are. This skill of sorting, summarizing, and explaining has valuable uses in every subject.

1. Students will participate in a group activity that will give them practice at writing "reader-based prose."

Objectives:

1. Each group will be asked to explain and describe in writing a map provided to them.

2. Each group will read their description aloud while other members of the class attempt to match it with one of the maps. This sharing exercise will expose the strengths and weaknesses of their descriptive pieces. Each group will then have a chance to revise their paper, making use of stronger descriptors and more definitive language than in the previous exercise.

3. Through the use of a wall map and discussion, students will explore the illegal drug problem in the United States. Students will brainstorm about the origins of illegal drugs and locate implicated countries on a map.

4. Students will then examine a map that presents visual information on the flow of heroin into the United States. Students will clarify terms that are related to the illegal drug economy.

5. Students will then create their individual informative written pieces explaining the map presented to them. Students will have a chance to share their writings and hear reactions from peers.

Materials Needed:

1. Copies of Handouts #3-#7: Continent Maps (one per group)
2. Transparency of a world map (prepared from the outline map, appendix G)
3. Copies of Handout #8: Map of Heroin Smuggling Routes
4. Wall Size World Map
5. Teacher Information Sheet on Illegal Drug Economy

Instructional Strategies:

Day 1

1. Divide the class into five groups. Each group should choose a spokesperson. Give each group one of the outline maps of the continents (Handouts #3-#7). Have students keep the maps to themselves and not permit other groups to see them.

2. Each group is then to describe in *writing* their continent with the following restrictions: *No proper nouns are to be used in their description*, i.e., names of oceans, rivers, mountains, etc. Students may use directions when describing coastlines and or relative positions (e.g., north of, southwest of, etc.). Each group has five minutes to complete the writing.

3. When students complete the writing task, place the transparency of the world map on the overhead projector. Each group spokesperson will have a chance to read his or her description. As a spokesperson reads a description instruct the students to write down the continents that fit this description. (Students should refer to the continents by letter only.)

4. Discuss the class's findings. Polling students will prompt them to rethink their writings. Use some of these key questions to assist students:
   a. How many maps fit group one's description? Group two's? Group three's? Group four's? Group five's?
   b. What made writing the descriptions difficult? Easy?
   c. What was the biggest frustration you had when writing your description?
   d. What assumptions did you make about your audience? What did you assume that they already knew about your map?
   e. If there was a good, detailed, and accurate description, use it as a model. What made this description so accurate? What words did the group use to make their description detailed and understandable to the other groups?

5. Have students reassemble in groups. Assign them the task of revising their descriptions. Give students further instructions to aid the process: What can you include in your description that will make it specific to your map? What details can

you add? Try using directions, mathematics terms, or some creative way to make your description unique from the others.

6. When the groups have revised their descriptions have them share again. Make use of the transparency to give the class a frame of reference.

7. Discuss and evaluate the newly drafted pieces.

Day 2

1. Hang wall map of the world prominently in front of the class.

2. Open discussion by asking for a definition of "illegal drugs." Students may also list those drugs classified in this category.

3. Lead class in a discussion of the origin of these illegal substances.

   a. Where in the world do these come from?

   b. Can you point out some of these countries on the map? Knowledge of specific countries is less important than knowing that most illegal drugs originate outside the United States.

4. Pass out copies of Handout #8. Have students read the explanatory paragraph found at the top of the page. Explain or clarify the following terms: capital investment, operating costs, retail network, import-export.

5. Assign writing task in this fashion: You have been given the job of writing a brief report for our school's P.T.A. or whatever parent-teacher organization the school might have. The P.T.A. is planning a special meeting for parents and students on Drugs in our Schools—Solving the Problem. Your report is part of the informative section of the meeting to provide data on the origin of illegal substances in the United States. Your written piece will be included in a handbook that all parents and students in attendance will receive. Your report needs to be a concise, informative piece on this topic. Using the skills you acquired from the previous day's practice, write your report based on the information provided to you on the map-graph. Be sure it contains necessary details and descriptions that are accurate. Be careful not to assume that your reading audience is knowledgeable about the information you are providing.

Day 3

Optional: Have students reassemble in groups and share their written work for peer evaluation or collect papers for teacher evaluation.

Writing Skills:	Summarizing from Data; Formal Letter Writing
Global Issue:	United States/World Trade
World Region:	United States and the World
Class Periods Required:	3 Days

Rationale:

In writing reports, students generally call upon narrative or textual material from which to glean needed information. Research reporting, however, depends upon the skill of obtaining information from data presented in the form of charts, tables, diagrams, and graphs. In addition, all of us are expected at some point to be able to look at a graph or chart and draw conclusions, form opinions, and make judgments and decisions based upon the information contained therein.

America's trade deficit, although of staggering proportions, bears little significance to our youth. The following lesson is designed to help middle school students begin to grasp a few facts about that deficit, and thus draw some conclusions from them and express these to a member of Congress in a formal letter-writing style.

Objectives:

1. Given an exercise in "real" trade, students will experience the challenges of carrying out successful transactions in a free market.
2. Given a handout to use as a guide, students in small groups will examine data regarding United States/world trade activity.
3. Students will select five aspects of the United States/world trade activity that concern them.
4. Students will write a letter to a member of Congress stating their concerns and suggesting specific action(s).

Materials Needed:

1. Trade items to be brought by students from home
2. Copies of Handouts #9 and #10
3. Calculators will be helpful!

One day in advance, announce to students that the next day they will participate in a special activity involving trading. Request that all students bring from home *one* item they no longer want, that their parents approve of them trading away, and that they feel someone else *will* want. Set no value limitations, except money is not allowed.

Instructional Strategies:

Day 1

1. Have students display the items they have brought to trade. Inform students that whatever agreements they make are binding. If they give away an item, it may not be taken back. Verbal agreements or promises should be equally binding. Exchange of money may not occur. Set additional rules as desired to maintain order, but generally allow students to move freely about the room to carry out whatever trade agreements they can make. After five to six minutes, warn students that they have only two to three minutes remaining to complete their trading. Time limits may be adjusted according to student's level of participation and interest.

2. Once students have returned to their seats, have them display their possessions.

3. Debriefing: Ask students how they felt about the activity. Do they feel they came out better or worse than before the trade? Was anyone unable to trade? Why? Some students probably chose not to trade. Why? A few may have added items to boost the value of their original "product." What did they add? Did it help? What else could they have added? Who came out the best (The most popular? The "wealthiest" to begin with? The most persuasive?) Who came out worst (Those who had nothing to begin with? The shyest?)

4. Have students make comparisons of this activity with world trade. Introduce, and define if necessary, the terms "import" and "export." How are these terms related to trading? Using the activity, give examples of the two terms (i.e., Sharon "exported" her apple and "imported" a comic book.) Do some countries export low value items that do poorly against others? (e.g., Ecuador is the world's largest exporter of bananas. How many bananas would it take to buy a Toyota from Japan? What are the implications of this? Is it generally better to be able to export raw materials than manufactured goods?) This discussion and comparisons with the preceding activity should continue until student interest declines.

5. Have students write three to five conclusions about trading they have reached as a result of the activity or follow-up discussion. Have volunteers share their conclusions.

Day 2

1. Review the previous day's activity, having students reread the conclusions they drew from it.
2. Form students into small groups of three to four.
3. Provide each student with Handouts #9 and #10.
4. Have students look at the title of Handout #9 and ask a volunteer to explain the purpose of the data and what information each column gives.
5. Ask each small group to use the data to complete Handout #10. Individual answers may come from personal opinion or group discussion. Allow ample time for groups

to consider each part in some detail. Circulate among groups to answer questions and see that they remain on task.

6. Discuss each part as a total group, allowing individuals to volunteer relevant opinions and information. Where there are differences of opinion, allow all sides to be argued.

7. Have each student write three to five sentences, each stating a concern or question about United States trade. These should be drawn from personal opinion, group, or class discussion, and the data.

Day 3

1. Using the form for business or formal letters suggested by the students' English textbook, have students write a letter to the President (who prepares our federal budget) or a member of Congress (both senators and representatives vote to approve or revise the budget). The letter should:

   a. Briefly review data to support the students' position;

   b. State the students' concerns and opinions;

   c. Offer suggestions from the student, if possible. In other words, the letter should be clear, brief, and to the point. They may wish to consider the following format for the body:

   "Given that (data)...

   I am concerned (of the opinion) that (concerns)... Therefore, I would like to suggest (propose, request)"...

2. The inside and outside address should be as follows:

   (To the President of the United States:)

   President (first and last name of the President)

   The White House

   1600 Pennsylvania Avenue

   Washington, D.C. 20500

   Dear Mr. President, or Dear President Smith,

   Respectfully yours,

   Cordially yours,

   Sincerely yours,

(To a U.S. Senator:)

The Honorable (first and last name of the Senator)

U.S. Senate

Washington, D.C. 20510

(To a U.S. Representative:)

The Honorable (first and last name of the member of Congress)

U.S. House of Representatives

Washington, D.C. 20515

Dear Sir (or Madam); or Dear Senator or

Representative (last name):

Sincerely,

Respectfully,

Cordially,

3. Use peer-editing techniques to revise first drafts. Have students turn in revised drafts for teacher evaluation. Final letters should be mailed promptly. Replies, if any, may provide incentive for future discussions or bulletin board displays. Be sure students examine the form of the letters they receive. Are they the same as the ones they sent? What information do the letterheads include? What additional information about United States trade have students learned from these letters?

Writing Skills: **Report Writing Using Primary Source Material; Classification Techniques for Gathering Information**

Global Issue: **Education**

World Region: **Japan/United States**

Class Periods Required: **2-4**

Rationale:

By the time students reach the middle school, most will have had experience in report writing. Typically, however, their research will have consisted of searching out secondary source material in encyclopedias and non-fiction sections of the library. A valuable experience for students, and one that will become increasingly useful as their education advances, is to have them cull needed information from primary source material. The following activities draw upon testimony before a U.S. Senate subcommittee by a Japanese male who has experienced both Japanese and American education, and current data on public education in Japan and the U.S. From this material, students will practice skills of summarizing, synthesizing, comparing, contrasting, and finally, preparing a report on Japanese versus American education.

Improving America's educational system based upon highly publicized comparisons with other developed countries is a heated issue in political circles. Students, through these activities, will be encouraged to make some judgments on their own about education and whether change is needed. Teachers using this material may wish to supplement the material provided with *A Nation at Risk* (National Commission on Excellence in Education. *A Nation at Risk: The Imperative for Educational Reform.* Washington, D.C.: U.S. Government Printing Office, 1983) and similar documents which address concerns regarding American education so that students can become familiar with the background of education as a national political issue.

Objectives:

1. Through a simulated hearing, students will read testimony presented before a senate committee by a high school student and through discussion, analyze information contained therein.

2. Students will use classification skills to compare and contrast Japanese and American education.

3. Optional: Students will analyze data presented in charts and graphs to gather additional information about Japanese and American schooling.

4. Students will use information gathered to prepare a report comparing and contrasting selected aspects of Japanese and American education.

Materials Needed:

1. Copies of Handout #11 and #12 for each student.
2. Optional: Teachers may wish to provide additional charts and graphs comparing U.S. and Japanese education (see Appendices A-F for examples).

Instructional Strategies:

Day 1

1. Organize students into informal groups of four to six and have each group decide on three goals of education in the United States. You may wish to get them started by telling them that "universal" public education in the United States had its beginning even before independence from Britain and that students have been *required* to attend school to age sixteen in most states since the beginning of this century. Why? (Most students have confronted parents and teachers with this question at some time! Therefore, this should be an effective start for a discussion.) What has led our great leaders to think it a good idea for all of our citizens to go to school? Thomas Jefferson said, "Above all things, I hope the education of the common people will be attended to; convinced that on their good sense we may rely with the most security for the preservation of a due degree of liberty." Ronald Reagan is quoted as saying, "A school is four walls with the future inside." What did they mean by this? What was Thomas Jefferson's goal for universal education? What was Reagan's goal? Do all nations share the same goals? How might they differ and why? List responses on the chalkboard and allow discussion of these. Have class choose the five most important.

2. The following procedures will help you recreate the senate hearing.

   a. Arrange your classroom so that there is a "head table."

   b. Inform the students that for the next two days they are going to re-enact a hearing before a senate committee in the United States Congress that actually took place on January 14, 1987. The hearing took place before the Senate Committee on Labor and Human Resources whose job is to review national goals in education. The committee is attempting to respond to recent criticism of our schools that has been directed primarily at high school education and that has pointed to our students' unfavorable showing on standardized tests compared with students from such countries as West Germany, Great Britain, and Japan. Among a large number of speakers invited to address the committee was a young man named Shin Murakami of Japan. Mr. Murakami has attended both Japanese and American high schools. His testimony will be the core of the following activity.

   c. Provide Handout #11 for each student. Ask strong readers to assume the roles of "the Chair" of a senate committee reviewing national goals in education and "Shin Murakami." They should sit at the head table. Tell students that they will re-enact the senate hearing, the classroom is now a senate chamber, and they are the U.S. senators serving on the "Committee on Labor and Human Resources." The date is January 14, 1987. The place is, of course, Capitol Hill, Washington, D.C.

d. You will need to assign the additional roles of Senator Stafford and Senator Harkin. These students should remain seated among the other "senators."

e. Inform students they must write a report to send to their state constituents informing them of the committee's findings, including a comparison and contrast of education in Japan and the United States, and it should come directly from this hearing. Therefore they will be given the text of the testimony, and as the proceedings take place, they may wish to make notes and underline portions of the text for future reference. Remind students that they will want to provide a clear and accurate report to interested citizens in their home state. They may want to be re-elected some day and poor communication with voters will hurt them.

f. Have "actors" read through the text of the hearing as if reading a play script. Encourage all students to think of themselves as important "players" in an important governmental proceeding, and to give as much attention to proceedings as they would hope the elected members of our nation's government would do.

g. Following the initial reading, group students in "subcommittees" to review the testimony. Handout #12 may be used as a guide.

3. On the chalkboard, draw a large chart similar to the one below:

Differences		Similarities
Japanese Schools	United States Schools	Both Systems

Have volunteers from the class name any school characteristics (U.S. or Japanese) discussed in Mr. Murakami's testimony. Select another student to name the column where that characteristic belongs. If a disagreement ensues, ask students to locate the portion(s) of the testimony that discusses the characteristic was discussed to clarify it. Proceed in like manner until students run out of ideas. If students feel that their own experience or knowledge conflicts with Mr. Murakami's testimony, they should resolve these feelings. For example, Mr. Murakami indicates that, "In Japan there is no getting out of being prepared...if you are to succeed," implying that in American schools such is not the case. Students should understand that the difference is not an either/or issue but a matter of *degree*. Most students in the United States are not expected to have already mastered the *next* day's assignment, whereas in Japan, teachers expect this level of preparation. Many of Mr. Murakami's statements thus reflect of differences by degree rather than in the extreme.

4. Optional: Distribute charts and data on appendices A-F. Have students discuss this information in small groups. Where information conflicts with Mr. Murakami's testimony, students must rely on judgment or further research.

5. Assimilating all the information gained from testimony, notes, additional data (if used); and discussion, students will write a report to "publish" in their respective states comparing and contrasting Japanese and American education. They may include personal knowledge and opinions if desired, remembering that they should present as much evidence as possible to support these. An effective report, however, should be predominantly objective and provide as much information as possible. If any students indicate a desire to do additional research, they should be encouraged to do so. Resources might include:

   a. The library

   b. Japanese people living the community

   c. School Board personnel, including administrators and Board members

   d. International Society for Educational Information, Inc.

   Koryo Building
   18 Wakaba 1-Chome
   Shinjuku, Tokyo 160
   JAPAN

   e. U.S. Department of Education

6. First drafts of reports may be peer-edited before the students write their final drafts. Final drafts should take the form of a congressional report to constituents, allowing for such statements as, "My fellow Ohioans,..."

Writing Skills:	Analyzing Information; Writing to Persuade
Global Issue:	Hunger
World Region:	Worldwide
Class Periods Required:	3

Rationale:

Through popularized activist groups such as Save the Children, USA for Africa, and Band-Aid, the hunger issue has become recognized worldwide. The consciousness of millions has been raised to realize that for many around the world hunger is an everyday occurrence.

The frustrating thing about the hunger issue is the inability to find workable, permanent solutions. Hunger for many countries is a logistical problem involving geographic factors that restrict ability to grow life-sustaining food. Hunger may also be the result of conditions created by the people themselves or by other human activities or agencies. Accounts of farmers turning their food fields over to the growth of cash crops are not uncommon. Some multinational companies promote this activity that farmers welcome by the promise of a profitable future. Whatever the reasons, the stark reality remains that although a few countries of the world live in abundance, a multitude suffer from deprivation.

Ample evidence suggests that middle level students are at the most altruistic stage of their lives. Although they may not demonstrate this trait to friends, family, and teachers, we see this clearly in their rush to help the needy, the hungry, or the sick and injured, especially in faraway places. For example, it was the response from young teenagers that made "We are the World" so popular, and led to an outpouring of food aid to East Africa. This, then, is an excellent time to develop their skills of analyzing information, forming an educated opinion, and practicing the art of persuading others to see their point of view. This exercise provides an opportunity for students to write a letter to the editor that will provide the vehicle through which they can test those opinions and persuasive arguments.

Objectives:

1. Students will participate in a free-writing exercise, giving them an opportunity to verbalize an event in their lives that will help them identify with a global situation.
2. Students will read and analyze two written selections about global hunger and compare them to their own narratives. Students will circle words or phrases that contain "loaded" language that persuaded them to think in certain ways.
3. Students will analyze a world hunger map that will demonstrate the unequal patterns of food supplies throughout the world. Students will answer question

pertaining to the geographical patterns on the map that will spark the formation of opinions and cause students to begin seeking solutions.

4. Students will examine and interpret cartoons that satirize the hunger issue. Through these drawings students will have another opportunity to look at the inequality of food supplies in the world. The cartoons will serve as an additional agent to prompt personal reaction from the students.

5. Students will read a hypothetical article written in response to a Hunger Project. Students will respond to that letter by writing their own to the editor of their local newspaper.

Materials Needed:

Enough copies for each student of the following handouts:

a. #13: World Hunger a Growing Crisis Handout

b. #14: Hunger Maps Handout

c. #15: Hunger Cartoons Handout

d. #16: Editorial

Instructional Strategies:

Day 1

1. Have students use notebook paper or their journals for a free-writing exercise. Pose this situation to the class:

   I want you to take a few minutes to think back upon a time when you were truly *hungry*. Think of a time when your stomach just *ached* for something to eat! Maybe it was once when you first awoke—or perhaps just before lunch. Some of you may have experienced being on a diet and you thought you were starving to death! Do you have an ideas about being or feeling hungry? Now—take five minutes and write about those feelings on paper. Write as much as you can—take the entire five minutes to do so. Do not worry about spelling or mechanics now—just use this time to get *your* story on paper!

2. Once students have completed the writing exercise, ask for volunteers to share their experiences. Students may be eager to share theirs after they have heard a sample. The teachers may read of a personal experience with hunger and the reading may encourage the students to participate.

3. After students have completed reading their papers, pass out copies of handout #13. Have students silently read the articles. The teacher may choose a good reader to read one or both of the articles aloud.

4. Allow students to compare and contrast their stories with the articles. Use some of these questions as prompts for discussion:

   a. Have any of you experienced the symptoms described in the Oxfam article (Oxfam America. *Organizer's Guide*)? Weakness? Headache? What happens to those after you eat?

  b. Do you agree with the statement "the rhythm of our meals does not correspond to what our bodies actually need..." When do you eat, when you're hungry or at designated times?

  c. How do you think the child in the *Current Events* article feels? What do you suppose he thinks about most of the time? How does the child's story differ from yours? What makes the child's hunger different from yours?

5. Divide the class into small groups. Each group should have their individual copies of handout #13. Have groups circle words or phrases that were most descriptive—those words that persuaded them to think in a certain way.

6. Have groups discuss their choices and write them on the chalkboard. Have the class discuss why these words are "loaded." Their choices may include: "pain" "slow-moving cancer" "body begins to eat itself." Lead a discussion using these prompt questions:

  a. Why are these words so powerful?

  b. How did these words make you feel a certain way?

7. Summarize the day's lesson, emphasizing the difference between hunger as the students know it and hunger as starvation. Also emphasize the use of strong descriptive language as an important tool in writing.

Day 2

1. Pass out copies of handout #14. Let groups examine the map for a short period. After studying the map, evaluate the students' perception with these prompt questions:

  a. On what continent is our country? Into what category does it fall?

  b. What other continents are in the same category? What countries can you name on these continents?

  c. How many countries fall into the "adequate" category?

  d. How many continents have some or most of their land in the "below adequate" category? Was there a continent in this category that you did not expect to find?

  e. Are there similarities between the continents or countries that are in the same categories? Speculate on the cause for their position on the hunger map. Is it created by humans? Has it occurred because of the physical geography of the country?

  f. What do you think could be done about this inequality?

2. Pass out copies of handout #15 to the class. Give the class a few minutes to look at each cartoon. Use the following framework of questions to conclude what message is given by each cartoon:

a. What objects, people, or places can you identify in the cartoon? (literal explanation)

b. What written message can you see?

c. What do each of the objects, people, or places in the cartoon represent?

d. What message is the cartoon attempting to relate?

e. Do you agree or disagree with the message?

3. Redirect focus of the class with this transition: By now your minds have been bombarded with information about a world problem. You no doubt have ideas and opinions of your own about this issue. Shortly, you will have the chance to express your point of view. I will give you a copy of an article that could have appeared in the newspaper, and you will write a response to that article. Your letter will give you a chance to voice your opinion and to persuade others to join your side. Let's take a few minutes to read the article.

4. Pass out copies of handout #16. Have the class read the article silently. Follow reading with a short discussion using some of these prompt questions:

a. What point of view is the author trying to get across to his reader?

b. What words did the author use to persuade readers to agree with the position stated in the article?

c. Do you feel that the author is justified in making these statements? Explain your answer.

d. Does the hunger problem in the United States differ from those places the writer refers to as "distant parts of the world?" Explain your answer.

e. Do you agree or disagree with the author's point of view?

5. Assign the writing task with the following guidelines:

You have been given two sides to a world issue. Now it is time for you to begin composing your letter. Each of you will write a letter to the editor of the local newspaper in response to the article you just finished reading. You may choose either side of the issue you wish to support. Whichever you choose, your purpose is to voice your opinion *and* persuade others to join your side.

The audience for your writing will be your classmates (and the readers of the local newspaper). Your letter should be as long as necessary to express your views in a clear and concise manner. Address your letter to a newspaper and be sure to sign your name. Newspapers will not print letters sent anonymously or under pseudonyms.

Day 3

Have students share their written work for peer analysis and evaluation. You may wish to display them as "Letters to the Editor" for a bulletin board display, using newspaper editorial pages as backing paper.

Writing Skills:	**Writing a News Article; Understanding Bias**
Global Issue:	**Human Rights**
World Region:	**U.S., Third World**
Class Periods Required:	**3-4**

Rationale:

Objectivity versus subjectivity is often difficult for students to differentiate. Distinguishing between fact and opinion, identifying bias, and especially the challenge of writing objectively when one feels strongly for or against an issue require a great deal of practice. The following activities are intended to get students thinking and writing about incidents objectively. At the same time, they will examine issues of bias and human rights as matters of global concern and even try their hand at writing a news article from a particular point of view to see that bias plays an important role in reporting for a particular readership.

Students in the United States frequently find events and policies in other parts bf the world unacceptable, applying their own values, ethics, and morals, and the "rules" these imply, as well as their understanding of American democracy to the rest of the world. It is necessary that they realize there are political conditions that vary from our own and that have tremendous effects on events, decision-making, and human behavior elsewhere. Although they will not always agree with the effects of these variations, they need exposure to differing points of view in order to understand these political differences.

Objectives:

1. Having read and discussed samples of news articles written from opposing viewpoints, students will identify words and phrases that indicate biased, factual, and opinionated reporting.
2. Students will attempt to write an objective account of an event drawn from biased reports.
3. Students will read and discuss a first person account of an incident in which the global issue of human rights is central.
4. Taking both possible positions, students will write news reports of the incident for two newspapers from opposing viewpoints.
5. Students will then attempt to write an unbiased account of the incident, attempting to avoid expressing their own biases.

Materials Needed:

Copies of Handouts #17, #18a, and #18b for all students.

Instructional Strategies:

Day 1

1. Provide Handout #17 for all students.

2. Have one strong reader read the two article excerpts to the class, or divide students into groups of three to four, placing strong readers and strong writers in each. Then have a strong reader read the passages to his or her group. Groups will remain together for additional activities.

3. After reading the two passages, inform students that the two passages are fictional excerpts from two high school newspapers. Within their groups, have them complete activities 1 and 2 on their handouts and provide guidance for the discussion called for in activity 2.

4. Provide instruction to support activity 3 as is appropriate for your class.

Day 2

1. Provide Handout #18 (a and b) to all students. Students should be made aware that the first-person account they are about to read is true and is in the words of a real person. The countries involved have been given fictional identities in order to avoid having students generalize their disapproval of the actions of Larovina's government to all its citizens. Have students read the account silently, or have a strong reader read it aloud as others follow along.

2. Inform students that the writer was serving as a missionary in the country of Larovina from a church in another country. The reason he was tortured was because Larovinian leaders believed he had written and sent an article to a news magazine in his own country that strongly criticized the Larovinian government.

   The teacher should guide students to understand the implications of this. The following discussion should encourage students to think about the point of view of the Larovinian government officials. The aim is to get them to understand that the Larovinian officials, *according to their point of view,* feel that the actions they took in response to the missionary's article, were justifiable and in accordance with Larovinian policy. However, as students will no doubt conclude on their own, the human rights issue in question precludes the style of punishment he received.

3. Suggested discussion format:

   a. From Larovina's standpoint, what did the missionary do wrong?

   b. How did his article pose a threat to the Larovinian government? (It put Larovina in a bad light among foreign nations. Officials may have felt that through the missionary's influence, Larovinian citizens could become dissatisfied with their government eventually leading to its downfall. The government may have feared eventual revolution, violence, economic ruin, etc.).

   c. Some governments do not allow the same freedoms for citizens that others do. Should the missionary, who had volunteered to live in Larovina, be subject to

Larovinian laws and policies, or his own country's laws and policies? (Officially, anyone, even vacationing in a foreign country, is subject to that country's laws and policies.)

d. Governments differ not only as to the laws they enact but also in the ways they may impose punishments upon offenders. What was the missionary's punishment? By our standards, did it seem fair? Do Americans or aliens now living in America ever get subjected to torture? Why not? (This question can be answered in two ways. First, U.S. laws prohibit torture in any form as punishment for law or policy breakers. Secondly, move on to the next activity...)

4. Have students turn to Handout #18 and read the Universal Declaration of Human Rights. Explain that this is only a portion of the full Declaration that the United Nations adopted in 1948. Have students discuss briefly why certain countries, even though they are members of the United Nations deny certain rights to their citizens (unstable governments as well as stable ones that require very tight control over public life, maintain strict laws and very severe punishments. It is perhaps worth noting that both Larovina and the missionary's home country are members of the United Nations). Have students cite examples familiar to them. In fairness to the Larovinian populace, point out that the missionary's experience was at the hands of the Larovinian *government officials,* who are responsible for maintaining their country's security. Ask if they think all Larovinians would agree with the punishment he received. Do all government activities, even in our nation always have the full support of the people? (You may wish to mention the Bay of Pigs incident, Watergate, Vietnam, the Iran-Contra Affair, etc.)

5. Although students have limited information regarding the events leading up to the incident described, and what they do have is through secondary or tertiary sources, they should be able to begin thinking about how those events might have been reported from two very different points of view and for two very different readerships. Once you feel students are able to *understand* both points of view to some degree, even though they do not agree with both, challenge them with the following assignment:

Write two news articles about the missionary incident beginning with his writing of the article and ending with his deportation from Larovina. One should be for the official newspaper published daily by the Larovinian government. The second should be for the missionary's hometown newspaper.

Some students may realize immediately that they are confronted with the question of bias in news reporting. Encourage them to be as objective as possible, but to remember that they are writing from a particular point of view and that neither article should get them fired from their job as reporter for their respective publications!

Day 3

Have students return to their groups per Day 1. Instruct them to take turns reading the articles they wrote from both country's points of view. After each reading, group members should point out words and phrases used that indicate bias on both sides of the issue. *Note*: Since students will lean heavily on the human rights side of the issue, the may have difficulty recognizing bias in those articles written from the standpoint sympathetic to the missionary. The teacher should guide them to recognize that just because one *agrees* with a particular point of view does not mean no bias exists. The implication is that bias is not always a bad thing.

Their final assignment should be to write an unbiased article for a neutral country's newspaper. They should be cautioned that the information they have available to them, other than the articles they wrote, comes from the missionary's description of his experience and conclusions drawn from class discussion. Therefore, the only *real* knowledge they have about the incident is from one person's point of view and reflects only one incident in a series of events. Encourage the students to supply fictionalized names for people, places, etc., as needed, but otherwise to stick to facts as they have them. The length of the article should be of no concern. Rather, efforts to write without bias when one feels strongly about an event is the challenge.

Optional Follow-up Activities:

1. Have students create a bulletin board on bias that is divided into two sides. Let them place favorite articles from the preceding assignments on the appropriate sides.
2. Have students read portions of front-page articles from your local newspaper to determine if U.S. reports are able to avoid bias. From this, they should begin to recognize that one's culture, politics, etc., negate the possibility of absolute objectivity.

Writing Skills:	**Effective Use of Imagery; Poetry Writing**
Global Issue:	**Deforestation**
World Region:	**Global, Tropical Rain Forest Regions**
Class Periods Required:	**4 days**

Rationale:

Oxygen. All human and animal life need this precious element to survive on our planet. For most of us, this resource is rarely given a second thought. We assume limitless amount of this life-giving gas will always be available. The reality of the situation is quite the opposite. Many scientists believe our oxygen supply is in serious jeopardy. The world's entire atmosphere may hang in an uneven balance.

Rain forest. Where does this "tropical paradise" fit into the picture? The rain forest has been described as the "lungs of the world." The rain forest surrounding the Amazon River in South America produces half of the world's plant-generated oxygen. The rain forest's delicate balance of evaporation is vital to the current weather patterns not only humid tropics but also in the United States as well as elsewhere in the world. Evaporation is essential for precipitation. However, if evaporation exceeds precipitation in a region, droughts or arid landscapes will result. On the other hand, when precipitation exceeds evaporation in a region, we can expect conditions conducive to agriculture and to the growth of lush vegetation. The distinctive climax vegetation* of many of the regions that straddle the equator is the tropical rain forest.** So distinctive is this multi-layered canopy of vegetation, each with its own habitats and ecosystems that we refer to the climate in this region as a tropical rain forest climate—one that is characterized by precipitation that exceeds 2.4" every month for each month of the year and temperatures that are uniformly high all year, with the coolest month usually averaging above 64.4° F and the annual range of temperature between the warmest and coolest months less than 9° F. Obviously, in the tropical rain forest regions precipitation exceeds evaporation.

Destruction. Currently, the rain forests of the world are being destroyed at alarming rates. An area of rain forest the size of West Virginia is irreversibly destroyed

---

*The final, stable vegetation of a region that has developed at the end of an undisturbed succession of plants that have developed under the particular set of environmental conditions present. Such vegetation is in dynamic equilibrium with the environment including other ecosystems, such as its animal life.

**In this activity when we use the term rain forest, we are referring to tropical rain forests. Other rain forests, namely temperate rain forests also exist, in the middle latitudes, usually coinciding with the northern portions of west coast marine climates—in northwest U.S. and Canada along the Pacific coast, southwest Chile, and even in some sections of New Zealand. Their extent was also much greater in the past than today and many of these are feeling serious stress from the encroachment of commercial logging operations.

every year. With this destruction comes loss of oxygen, increase of carbon dioxide, and less rain. The tragic loss of plant and animal life is immeasurable. The potential of rain forest resources will be lost forever.

Concern. The most important aspect of this activity is the consciousness raising that will occur among middle level students. Students will be made aware of the situation regarding rain forest areas of the world. They will be made aware of some possible alternatives to this destruction. This exercise will motivate students to seek change.

Response. In response to this heightened awareness, students will be given the opportunity to create a poem expressing their knowledge and feelings about this issue. A loose structure combined with motivational activities will provide the framework for this creative writing activity.

Objectives:

1. Students will be able to list personal and scientific knowledge about a forest through the use of a brainstorming exercise.
2. Students will compare and contrast their descriptions of a forest with descriptions of rain forests found in the tropical areas of the world.
3. Students will engage in free-writing, by compiling response lists in answer to a series of sensory stimuli questions about the rain forest.
4. Students will be able to identify the location and geographical characteristics of the rain forest.
5. Given resources, students will be able to cite statistics on the diversity of plant and animal life found within the rain forest.
6. Students will be able to list the immense variety of products that are derived from the natural resources found in the rain forest.
7. Students will be able to cite statistics on the rate of current destruction of the rain forest.
8. Students will be able to list the two main causes for the destruction of the rain forest.
9. Students will analyze a political cartoon, interpreting its social commentary on the destruction of the forest.
10. Students will read and compare poetry examples looking for patterns and metaphors.
11. Students will create their own poem in response to the information revealed about the rain forest and the feelings this issue arouses.

Materials Needed:

1. Class set of handouts #19-25.

Instructional Strategies:

Day 1

1. Gather class together for brainstorming. Use the chalkboard to record answers from the students during the activity.

2. Prompt students with these questions:

   a. When I say the word "forest," what is the first word that enters your mind?

   b. What memories, feelings, experiences, or thoughts come to your mind when hear the word "forest"? Allow students enough time to generate answers that include animals, plant life, sights, sounds, physical sensations, or emotions that are all part of their knowledge or memories of the forest. You should also encourage students to offer fictional characters or events from books.

3. Summarize students' responses. Have students generalize about the answers they offered. Ask: Can we conclude that the forest is a happy place? A place for life? Silent? or noisy? Living? or stagnant? Students should conclude that the forest is a place of life, growth, and enchantment for the world.

4. Pass out Handout #19. Allow time for students to read silently.

5. Use these questions to obtain student reactions and ensure understanding:

   a. What made these descriptions of the forest similar to ours? Pick out words in the article that has the same meaning as the ones we chose.

   b. What made these descriptions different?

   c. What did you learn about the forest that you did not know before this activity?

6. Tell the class they are going to write about visual images that appear in their minds when they hear some questions. For some students closing their eyes will help them to block outside stimuli and aid in concentration. Read the following questions slowly, allowing students time between each question to write their answers. Student answers need not be in sentences, but may be a collection of thoughts and phrases.

   What things look like a rain forest? What things sound like a rain forest? What things smell like a rain forest? How does the thought of a rain forest make you feel? What things taste like a rain forest? What experiences or ideas seem like a rain forest? Can you think of places that remind you of a rain forest?

   When students have completed this exercise have them *save their sheets*. These will be very helpful when students are ready to begin their poetry composition.

Day 2

1. Pass out Handout #20. Introduce the map to the class by informing students that the forests described in the previous handout can be found in the shaded areas of the map. They are referred to as rain forests because of their position, make-up, and life within. Use these questions to emphasize some geographical points:

    a. What continents do you see that have a rain forest?

    b. Can you name some countries on these continents where these rain forests exist?

    c. At what elevations are rain forests found? What latitudes? What are their climatic characteristics? Can be generalize that all rain forests are at low latitudes, low elevations, and have hot, moist climates?

2. Pass out Handout #21. Allow students to read silently or choose a reader for the class. These readings will allow the students to realize the vast variety of plant and animal life that lives in the forest.

3. Prompt discussion of the readings with these key questions:

    a. What type of statistics can you give about the animal and plant life in the forest?

    b. Were you amazed at the number of plants and animals that are found in the forest. Name some of them.

    c. What other curious facts did you learn about these plants and animals and their environment?

Day 3

1. Begin class with this introduction: We have discovered over the past few days that a forest is far more than a place we may take a hike or the perfect setting for a fairy tale. The forest is a place of life and growth for thousands of species of plants and animals on earth. In fact, there is so much life that scientists are just beginning to discover the complex world of the rain forest. Every year people are destroying *fifty million acres of tropical rain forest*—that is, about the area as large as the state of Oregon. By conservative estimates, *twenty-seven acres are completely destroyed each minute.* In the fifteen minutes it takes your parents to drink a cup of coffee in the morning, *135 acres of rain forest disappear.* Virtually all our rain forests will be gone by the year 2032—only 45 years from now. Some of you may be having these thoughts: What does this all mean to us? Who cares? Can't the world do without one less animal or plant? What differences does it make for us—we live in the United States? Where there are no rain forests anyway!

2. Pass out Handout #22. The class may read silently or choose a reader to read aloud. Introduce the reading in this manner: "Through these readings we will discover the importance of the rain forest—how the rain forest, though thousands of miles away, affects our lives."

3. Inform students that in addition to the products and life forms that rain forests provide, they also provide oxygen, vital to the air we breathe. The rain forest surrounding the Amazon in South America, for example, is said to produce half the plant-generated oxygen *in the world!* Rain forests are described as "the lungs of the world." Discuss with students why this is important and what implications it

has for humans all over the world...even those who live far away from these rain forests.

4. Evaluate students' understanding of the texts with these questions:

   a. Name five products that come from the rain forest.

   b. Which of these (or others) amazed you because of its origin?

   c. Which products could possibly save our lives or the lives of future persons?

   d. Is there any one product that we could do without? (Students may need to do some research to find answers to this questions.)

5. Write these phrases on the chalkboard: "Commercial Logging," "Beef Cattle Ranching." Introduce these items by saying: "You are looking at the top two reasons for the destruction of the rain forest. Loggers in their search for usable trees clear entire forests looking for hardwoods. Only 10% of the trees in the rain forest are usable, but loggers choose to clear entire forests instead of taking the time and expense to gather only commercially valuable trees. The insatiable appetites of many humans for beef is the cause of a second reason for the destruction of the rain forest. Cattle ranchers pay people to cut down the forests to make room for the cattle to graze. Once the trees are removed, the poor soil at the surface of the rain forest can maintain pasture grasses for only a few years. Once the soil is depleted the cattle ranchers move on to another area, thus destroying more forest. It has been said that for every quarter-pound hamburger that is eaten, fifty-five square feet of rain forest was destroyed to obtain."

6. Pass out Handout #23. Have students study it for a moment. Realize that the cartoon is possibly going to create controversy over its reference to the theory of evolution. If necessary, cover or cut away "ancestral man" before reproducing. The point can still be made. Lead a discussion of this handout with these questions?

   a. What scientific theory is this cartoon showing?

   b. What happened to the last man?

   c. What is the symbolism of the chain saw held by the last man?

   d. What message is this cartoon trying to communicate?

Day 4

1. Pass out Handout #24 (poetry examples) to the class. Introduce these in the following manner: "All of these poems have something in common. They follow a similar format or pattern in the way they were created. Let's read them together and try to discover that pattern." Have the class read the poems silently or aloud. Follow with these discussion questions:

   a. What senses were used to describe the subject of the poetry?

   b. What "unusual" comparisons were made between the subject of the poem and the senses? Give an example.

    c. What kind of pattern do you see in these poems?

2. Have students refer to their answers written in response to Handout #20. Pass out Handout #20 and #25 to the class. Set the students to their writing task in this manner: "You will have your chance today to become a poet! Many great poems have been written in response to passionate feelings: love, sorrow, joy, hate. Some of you may be having those same kinds of feelings on the peril of the rain forest. Use those feelings to create your message—your poem. In front of you is a list of responses that you wrote to answer the questions in Handout #20. Each of those answers describe an emotion or sense when thinking of the rain forest. Handout #25 gives you a pattern to follow to create your poem. Use that pattern as a basis to write your poem. Some of you may want your poem to describe a rain forest as it should be in nature. Some of you may want your poem to help stop the destruction of the forest. You may need to go back to your lists and add new feelings and senses you have felt since you have received additional information. Use the questions in Handout #20 to help you. Most importantly, let your poem speak your heart and your mind—Create!!"

Writing Skills:	Writing a Summarized Biography; Creative Problem Solving
Global Issue:	General
World Region:	General
Class Periods Required:	1-2

Rationale:

Change and hope are two processes that are intrinsically linked with the individual's thoughts about the future. One struggles to make change and hopes that it will make a difference—one hopes for a change that will make the world a better one in which to live. These two actions seem to have a cyclical relationship—each sparking the other.

Humanity faces many issues that threaten the existence of life on our planet; some that threaten the survival of the planet itself. Individuals wage a constant battle with the dangers of modern existence: war, famine, drugs, loss of freedom and dignity, destruction of the environment, etc. At times these conflicts seem too enormous for any one generation to solve. Thus, we rely on hope and change to bring about solutions against what seems to be overwhelming odds. Yet as long as we cling to hope, we are able to keep on struggling for change.

Middle level students also need to believe in the power of hope and change. When they confront"impossible" problems they often become discouraged and frustrated. Some, when faced with overwhelming challenges choose to "drop out." It may seem more reasonable to retreat from problems than to confront them. Indifference allows for an easy escape and, sadly, an alternative to hope and change.

This exercise permits middle level students the opportunity to be creative, even revolutionary or wildly imaginative, to pursue a course of action of their choosing to solve a world problem. This is a highly personal effort and should receive full support of the teacher. The solution(s) they create, no matter how unrealistic, how great, or how simple, will reward the student with a feeling of hope and the knowledge that it is the effort of the individual that often makes a difference between the status quo and improvement in our lives.

Objectives:

1. Students will participate in group discussion to examine samples of fictional obituaries in order to create a useful definition of the term.

2. Students will again examine the obituaries closely, identifying the form and function of the writing within each piece.

3. Students will practice this style of writing by creating their own obituary that will immortalize their life and their specific contribution to the world.

Note:

For students to feel the full effect of this lesson, you should use it as a culminating exercise to the lessons contained in this booklet. As students have explored the world with its many complexities, they may have experienced feelings of frustration concerning the problems and elusive solutions to world issues. We hope this exercise will alleviate that frustration giving students a positive feeling about their power as individuals in the world.

Materials Needed:

1. Copies of Handouts #26 and #27 for each member of the class.
2. Blank, white paper for student obituaries.

Day 1

1. Begin class with a discussion of obituaries. Have students offer definitions. (Be sure to have students conclude that an obituary contains a summarized biography of a person's life.)

2. Pass out handout #26. Give students time to read samples silently or ask volunteers to read each sample aloud.

3. Discuss the samples with the class. You may want to use some of these questions:
   a. What did you learn about each of the people?
   b. Which ones were more detailed than others?
   c. Why did the writer include the information provided?
   d. What purpose does an obituary serve?

4. Have students examine the writing carefully:
   a. What types of facts did the writer include?
   b. How is the writing in an obituary presented? Factual? Emotional?
   c. Why would the writer present an obituary in this manner?

5. Assign writing task to the class. Use this prompt to define clearly their purpose in writing:

   "Throughout the past_____, we have been using our writings to serve two purposes: (1) to learn and practice different skills and types of writing and (2) to improve our global awareness of the world around us.

   Throughout our discoveries you may have at times felt feelings of frustration with the enormity of the problems at hand. Many of the global issues that we discussed seem to have no conceivable solution. Some of these concerns seem so complex it would take a million ideas to generate one answer!

   As individuals, you will have the opportunity today to use your creativity to solve a world problem. You will be taking an imaginary journey to the end of your life. Think for a moment—it is twenty, forty, seventy years in the future—

you are gone now, but your memory remains for you have made a very important contribution to the world. All of you are given the unique opportunity to write your own obituary! Yours will tell the unique tale of your life: who you are and why you are important."

6. Hand out copies of Handout #27, if desired, to aid students in creating the obituary.

7. Evaluate and display.

HANDOUTS

Handout #1

Name_____

Read the following scenario. Select persons from your group to play:

1.   Four (4) children for side A
2.   Four (4) children for side B
3.   Mrs. DeKamp, a neighbor

Wad up paper, if desired, to serve as snowballs.

Two groups of children are having a snowball fight across a driveway separating two front yards. An elderly woman, Mrs. DeKamp, is walking slowly up the street toward the children carrying a sack of groceries. Mrs. DeKamp is a favorite neighbor, for she is forever smiling, speaks to everyone, and always seems to have a plate of cookies handy to offer children who stop by to swing on her porch railing and share the day's news.

Suddenly the children facing her see her stumble, losing her grip on the sack and spilling the contents into the snow. The snowball fight is forgotten as the children race to help her gather her purchases. One gallant youngster carries her sack to her home while the rest surround her with chatter accompanying her to her door.

Once certain she is safely inside, the opposing sides return to their mild name-calling and the snowball fight resumes with increased fury.

Handout #2

Catholics, Protestants Loved Scruffy the Dog—and He's Gone

by Donald O'Higgins

Londonberry, Northern Ireland (UPI)—Scruffy is missing and presumed dead.

That bald statement may not cause a flutter in the sophisticated capitals of the world but in Londonberry it has cast a gloom as much as the city's famous siege walls.

In the Catholic Creggan ghetto housing estate they just will not accept it. In the Protestant Waterside area, dismay and disbelief greeted the news along the grapevine.

"Nothing will be the same without Scruffy," said Tom McGinty in a Creggan bar, gently tilting his Guiness from side to side in a pint tumbler. "Scruffy stood with us during the roughest times."

"Aye," agreed a youth sipping vodka. "Scruffy was a dog in a million. With Scruffy gone there's no fun in aggro (fighting) any more.

Even in the British army barracks, where stiff upper lips were the order of the day, the odd quiver could be discerned."

"Scruffy was not just any dog," said a young captain and was bewildered, "Scruffy was…well, he was…damn it, man. He was Scruffy."

News that Scruffy was missing first came from local photographer Willie Carson, whose camera followed the dog on many an escapade.

"He's gone. I'm afraid he's dead. He must be,"Carson said.

Shock, disbelief, then gradual acceptance that Scruffy hadn't been around for some time spread through the ancient city.

Scruffy was no ordinary dog. He never seemed to claim a permanent home or owner. He was totally non-sectarian, bestowing his favors on Catholics, Protestants and British troops in equal measure.

No one seemed to know with certainty when he arrived in the city and became an integral part of the riot scene.

In appearance, he seemed to be the product of some chance meeting between an amorous collie and a terrier of sorts. The end product could have been unseemly were it not for Scruffy's near-human lopsided grin. He was tousled-haired, slightly squint-eyed, forever tail-wagging, and a riot chaser without equal.

At the clump of the first rock off an army vehicle, Scruffy would be there dancing on his hind legs, his body quivering with excitement.

In one particularly nasty riot when British troops were drenching the Bogside Catholic ghetto with nauseous gas, a perplexed army sergeant turned to his captain and said in amazed tone, "blimey, sir,would you look at that."

He pointed to Scruffy delightedly sniffing the cannisters and wagging his tail.

"The ruddy mut seems to love it," the sergeant said. "The ruddy Irish, even their dogs are mad."

On another occasion Scruffy stopped a riot.

It was in full swing when the whisper went around. "Scruffy is trapped."

Youths dropped bricks and bottles and ran toward a burning building.

"What are they up to now," asked a puzzled and suspicious British officer.

"Scruffy's trapped," shouted a youth over his shoulder.

"What's that?" said the British officer, his face stiffening with anxiety.

"Scruffy's inside," said the youth, pointing to smoke billowing form the blazing house.

"Come on,"yelled the captain. He raced away followed by his troops toward the building.

"There he is," they shouted.

On the window ledge stood Scruffy upstairs in the two-story house.

"Get a ladder," yelled someone. "Scruffy cocked his head sideways, with the familiar lop-sided grin and waited, tail wagging.

Young Martin Harkins, a local amateur boxer, himself to die later, scramble up the ladder and brought Scruffy to safety.

The cheers rang out over the city. The captain and his men withdrew. The rioters reformed. The stones began to whiz again. The riot was on.

And there in the middle, happily trying to catch rubber bullets on the bounce, was Scruffy.

But now Scruffy has gone. Perhaps to another city where the action is faster. Perhaps run over in the dark of night.

Who knows?

But his loss cannot be put into words. Only those the world over who have ever owned and loved a Scruffy know how Tom McGinty feels as he gazes into his Guinness.

Handout #3

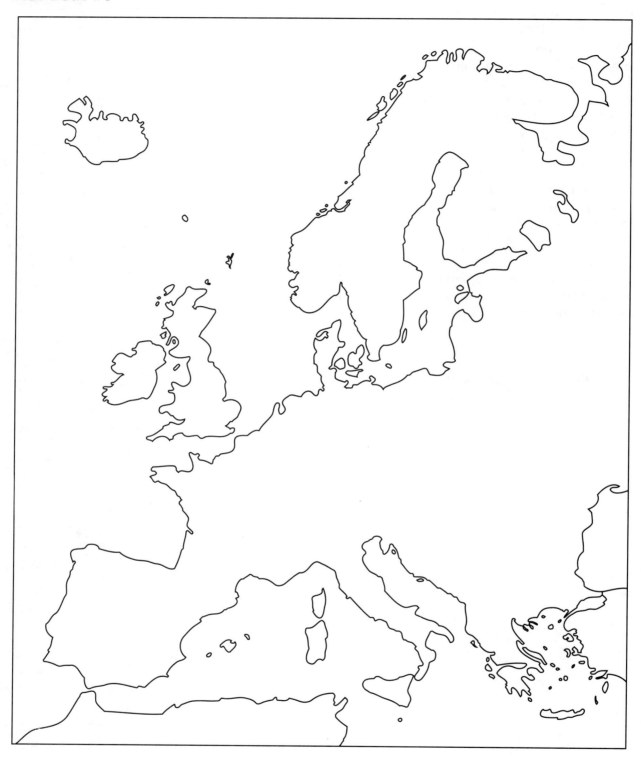

Handout #4

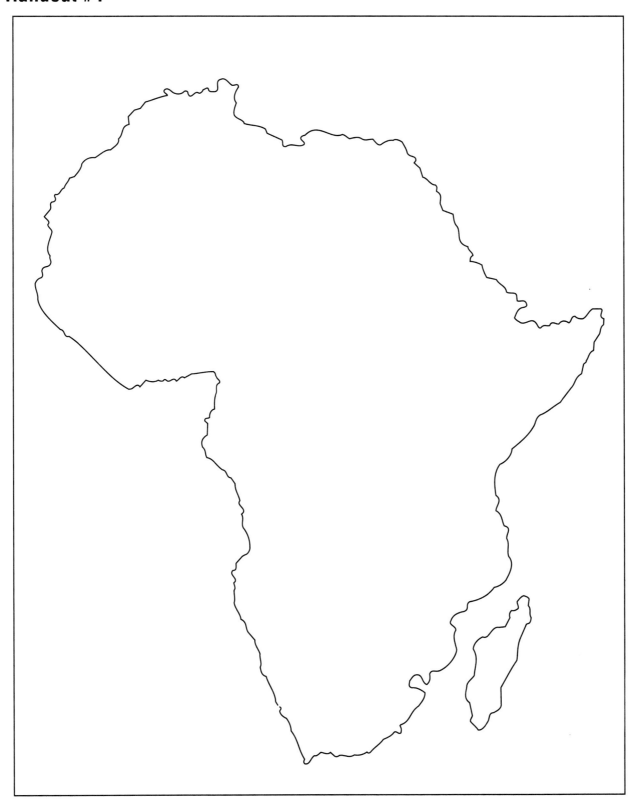

Handout #5

Handout #6

Handout #7

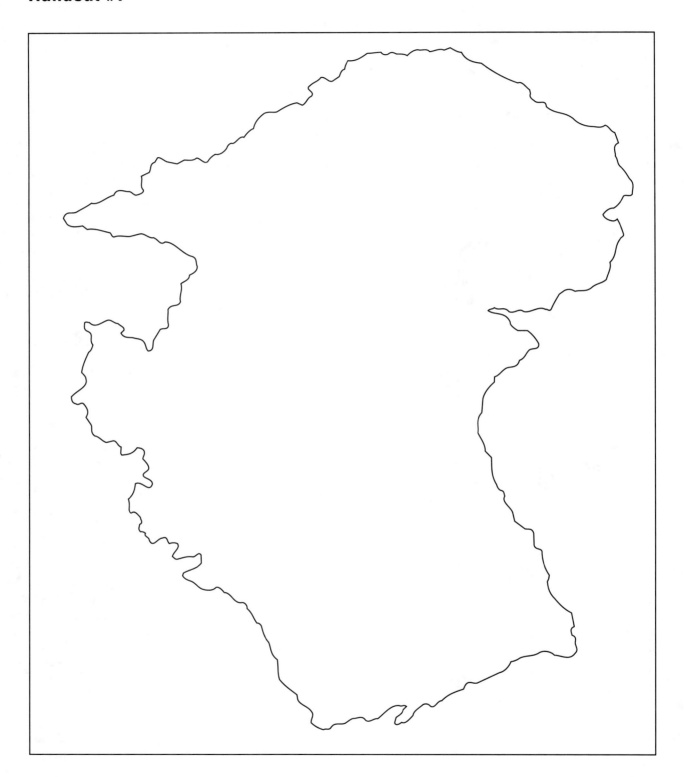

Handout #8

The Illegal Drug Economy in the U.S.: $50 Billion Gross Retail Value in 1985

"...Illegal drugs are classified by the Controlled Substance Act into four categories: 1) cannabis (e.g. marijuana and hashish); 2) cocaine; 3) dangerous drugs (e.g., methamphetamine, LSD, methaqualone, and amphetamines); and opiates (e.g., heroin). The size of the illegal economy supported by the three drugs (marijuana, cocaine, and heroin) that are the focus of this study (because they are mostly or entirely imported) are estimated by OTA to have had an annual gross retail value of about $50 billion. Thus, the retail sales of marijuana, cocaine, and heroin equal the combined sales of the Nation's two largest retailers, Sears and K-Mart. Unlike Sears and K-Mart, the drug industry requires small capital investment, involves no retail stores, and minimal investment in production and storage facilities. The industry's major operating costs are associated with paying employees and supporting (its) illegal transportation network..."

Heroin Smuggling Routes from Source Areas to the United States

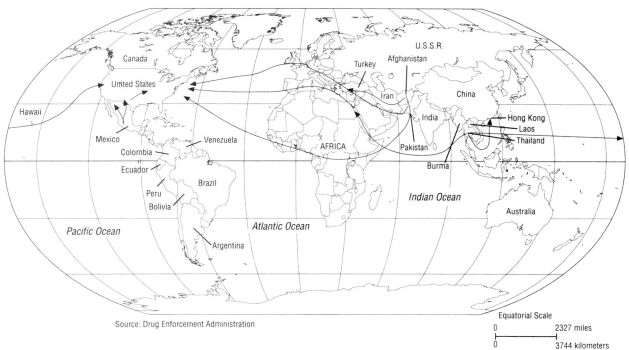

Source: Drug Enforcement Administration

Equatorial Scale

0 — 2327 miles

0 — 3744 kilometers

Handout #8

The Illegal Drug Economy in the U.S.: $50 Billion Gross Retail Value in 1985

"...Illegal drugs are classified by the Controlled Substance Act into four categories: 1) cannabis (e.g. marijuana and hashish); 2) cocaine; 3) dangerous drugs (e.g., methamphetamine, LSD, methaqualone, and amphetamines); and opiates (e.g., heroin). The size of the illegal economy supported by the three drugs (marijuana, cocaine, and heroin) that are the focus of this study (because they are mostly or entirely imported) are estimated by OTA to have had an annual gross retail value of about $50 billion. Thus, the retail sales of marijuana, cocaine, and heroin equal the combined sales of the Nation's two largest retailers, Sears and K-Mart. Unlike Sears and K-Mart, the drug industry requires small capital investment, involves no retail stores, and minimal investment in production and storage facilities. The industry's major operating costs are associated with paying employees and supporting (its) illegal transportation network..."

Teacher Information Sheet

Some International Figures on Narcotics

Background:

Narcotics abuse and trafficking are serious problems that have begun to plague developing as well as industrialized nations. Producing and trafficking countries, once immune from the effects of narcotics, now face growing addict populations of their own. Like Western Europe and the US, these newly affected countries are exploring ways to fight back, realizing that narcotics are not only health concerns but threats to national and international security.

World Drug Supply:

Illicit production of opium, marijuana, and cocaine far exceeds worldwide demand. According to 1986 estimates, narcotics production was up all over the world. Opium production in the "Golden Triangle" of Southeast Asia was estimated at 820-1,415 metric tons: Burma produced 700-1,100 metric tons, and Laos produced 100-290 metric tons—substantial increases over the levels of recent years. The "Golden Crescent" nations of Pakistan, Afghanistan, and Iran produced 740-1,060 metric tons of opium in 1986. War-torn Afghanistan actually grew the bulk of this opium—an estimated 400-500 metric tons were produced in Iran. Defying governmental efforts to end production, Pakistani farmers cultivated some 140-160 metric tons of opium.

Mexico is thought to be the world's singular largest cultivator of marijuana, producing between 4,000 and 6,000 metric tons in 1986. Colombia, Jamaica, and Belize also were major marijuana producers, bringing the estimated world supply of marijuana to between 9,365 and 13,405 metric tons.

Coca cultivation remained very high during 1986, when the world supply of coca leaf reached between 152,000 and 188,320 metric tons. Peru produced 95,000-120,000 metric tons of leaf, and Bolivian cultivation was estimated at 44,000-52,920 metric tons. Colombia produced roughly 12,000-13,600 metric tons of coca leaf. Most of the region's coca is refined into cocaine in Colombia.

U.S. Problems:

Approximately 95% of the narcotics consumed in the U.S. are imported. All of the cocaine used by Americans originates in the Latin American countries of Peru, Bolivia, and Colombia, while heroin is derived from the opium poppy grown in Southeast and Southwest Asia and Mexico. Most of the marijuana smoked by Americans is grown in this hemisphere. Although recent statistics indicate that Americans' marijuana use has decreased and heroin use has stabilized (at about 500,000 heroin addicts), there is still an alarmingly high rate of experimentation with cocaine by Americans and regular use is growing here and in Europe.

Increasing Demand:

The number of addicts in drug producing and trafficking countries has increased dramatically over the past 5 years. Pakistan, with no reported heroin addicts in 1980, now has 400,000-500,000. Bolivia estimates that 100,000 of its young people are addicted to "basuco," a smokable interim stage in cocaine refining..."

Source: Excerpted from a May 1987 issue of *Gist* ("International Narcotics Control"), U.S. Department of State, Bureau of Public Affairs.

Handout #9

The Top Purchasers of U.S. Exports and the Top Suppliers of U.S. Imports

Top 50 Purchasers of U.S. Exports in 1986 Millions of Dollars 1986		Top 50 Suppliers of U.S. Imports in 1986 Millions of Dollars 1986	
Canada	45,333	Japan	85,457
Japan	26,882	Canada	68,662
Mexico	12,392	Germany, West	26,128
United Kingdom	11,418	Taiwan	21,251
Germany, West	10,561	Mexico	17,558
Netherlands	7,847	United Kingdom	16,033
France	7,216	Korea, South	13,497
Korea, South	6,355	Italy	11,312
Australia	5,551	France	10,586
Taiwan	5,524	Hong Kong	9,474
Belgium/Luxembourg	5,399	Brazil	7,340
Italy	4,838	Venezuela	5,446
Brazil	3,885	Switzerland	5,367
Saudi Arabia	3,449	China	5,241
Singapore	3,380	Singapore	4,884
Venezuela	3,141	Sweden	4,637
China	3,106	Netherlands	4,363
Hong Kong	3,030	Belgium/Luxembourg	4,191
Switzerland	2,976	Saudi Arabia	4,054
Spain	2,615	Indonesia	3,675
Israel	2,239	Spain	2,956
Egypt	1,982	Australia	2,873
Sweden	1,871	Nigeria	2,681
Malaysia	1,730	Malaysia	2,534
India	1,536	Israel	2,505
Ireland	1,434	South Africa	2,476
Philippines	1,363	India	2,465
Colombia	1,319	Philippines	2,150
USSR	1,248	Colombia	2,039
Turkey	1,160	Algeria	1,980
South Africa	1,158	Thailand	1,873
Indonesia	946	Denmark	1,869
Argentina	944	Ecuador	1,603
Norway	937	Norway	1,170
Thailand	936	Dominican Republic	1,138
Dominican Republic	921	New Zealand	1,097
New Zealand	881	Ireland	1,046
Pakistan	830	Finland	986
Chile	823	Argentina	938
Bahamas	761	Chile	935
Denmark	758	Austria	912
Panama	711	Peru	858
Peru	693	Trinidad & Tobago	840
Kuwait	657	Romania	839
Portugal	638	Angola	729
Ecuador	601	Costa Rica	720
Trinidad & Tobago	532	Yugoslavia	713
Yugoslavia	528	Turkey	690
Iraq	527	Guatemala	647
El Salvador	518	Iran	612

Handout #10

Name_____

You will find a calculator beneficial for the following activities:

1. To what five countries did the U.S. export the most goods in 1986? What was the total income to the U.S. from these?

_____

_____

_____

_____

_____

_____

    Total income _____

2. From what five countries did the U.S. import the most goods during 1986? What was the total expenditure for these?

_____

_____

_____

_____

_____

    Total expenditure _____

3. If you can, calculate the totals for all exports and imports. Compare income versus expenditure.

    Total income _____

    Total expenses _____

4. On a map, locate the countries with which we do the most trading.

5. With which countries did we maintain a trade balance? A trade surplus (our exports exceeded our imports)? A trade deficit (our imports exceeded our exports)? How many countries fall into each category?

    Balance _____

    Surplus _____

    Deficit _____

    Number of Countries in Each Category_____

6. What do you notice about our trade with the USSR? How do you explain this? What could you do to obtain an explanation?

_____

_____

_____

_____

7. What other questions do these data raise? How might you get answers?

_____

_____

_____

8. The national debt now exceeds two trillion dollars. Our country has had to borrow against itself in order to pay countries to whom we owe money. Discuss the following questions: Should we stop trading? What do we import that we absolutely have to have? What would happen to our foreign relations if we suddenly stopped buying goods from our friends?

9. What conclusions can you and your group draw about U.S. trade? In three to five statements, outline the concerns you have. What ideas can you suggest to ease the problem, if there is one?

    Concerns:

    a. _____

    b. _____

    c. _____

    d. _____

    e. _____

    Possible solutions or ways to lessen the problem:

    a. _____

    b. _____

    c. _____

    d. _____

    e. _____

Writing for a Global Perspective

Handout #11

The CHAIRMAN. Thank you very much.

Our next witness is a very important witness, Shin Murakami, who is a Japanese high school student. We are glad he is here today. There has been a great deal of discussion about education in Japan and the United States. It is interesting to hear from a student such as yourself, who has been in school in both countries.

Shin went to school in Japan from age six to ten; he has been in the United States from second through fifth grade, and eleventh and twelfth. So he was in the United States, then Japan, and then in the United States. He has had a very interesting educational experience. There has been a great deal of attention given to where we are as a country where Japan is, and where other countries are—not that what happens in other countries necessarily ought to be replicated here. But I think all of us can always learn from other people's experience in trying to apply some of the worthwhile and useful benefits of a program to see how they may or may not be suited to our own situation.

There have been many studies done, but we are very fortunate to have you here this morning. You are very good to come.

Are you missing school today?

Mr. MURAKAMI. Yes, I am.

The CHAIRMAN. You are. [Laughter.]

We met downstairs some of the guests that you brought with you. Do you have some of your teachers?

Mr. MURAKAMI. No; just my mother. There are some graduate students with Mr. Long.

The CHAIRMAN. Well, they are all very welcome here, too.

We are delighted to have you, and we hope you feel at home. We are very appreciative of your presence here.

STATEMENT OF SHIN MURAKAMI, STUDENT, WINSTON CHURCHILL HIGH SCHOOL, POTOMAC, MD

Mr. MURAKAMI. Thank you.

Mr. Chairman, members of the Committee on Labor and Human Resources, I am Shin Murakami, a twelfth-grade student who has been educated both in the United States and Japan. When I was in Japan, I attended Tamagawa Gakuen High School, located in Tokyo. Presently, I attend Winston Churchill High School, located in Potomac, Maryland. I am here today to share some of my observations about being a student in both the United States and Japan.

Being a student in Japan was quite different from being a student in the U.S. School would begin at 7:55 in the morning and go on until about 3:00. After this, every day of the school year, the students would clean the school. After cleaning the school, I would have basketball practice for two to three hours. The goal was to learn the discipline of the sport and not necessarily to enjoy it.

I believe that discipline plays a large role in Japanese society. Each evening, after two or three hours of after school activities and dinner, I would rush off to Juku, which is commonly known as "cram school" in the U.S. This is a private school which deals with only the academic courses. After about two hours of Juku, I would come home and at about 10:00 I would start my homework.

NATIONAL GOALS—EDUCATION

HEARING

BEFORE THE

COMMITTEE ON LABOR AND HUMAN RESOURCES UNITED STATES SENATE

ONE HUNDREDTH CONGRESS

FIRST SESSION

ON

REVIEWING NATIONAL GOALS IN EDUCATION

JANUARY 14, 1987

Printed for the use of the Committee on Labor and Human Resources

U.S. GOVERNMENT PRINTING OFFICE

WASHINGTON : 1987

74-573

For sale by the Superintendent of Documents, Congressional Sales Office
U.S. Government Printing Office, Washington, DC 20402

Juku is a very important part for any student who is preparing for the high school examinations.

The formal homework assignment which I would start at 10:00 was only a small part of what was required of me. Other than the homework, I would have to review the entire day's work, and I would have to preview the next day's assignments.

In Japan there is no getting out of being prepared or reviewing if you are to succeed.

Science and mathematics, I believe, are much more demanding in Japan. For instance, if you are taking a math course in the U.S., and you feel that you cannot keep up with it, then you would simply drop the course and take an easier course. In Japan, you are required to take the same mathematics course as anybody else in your grade. The pressure to succeed is very high. Some of my friends have been very confused as to how to handle their failure and its pressures.

Writing instruction is also demanding. In Winston Churchill High School, my teacher stresses writing creatively, creative writing; whereas in Japan, they would emphasize more on punctuation or grammar. Reading class in Japanese school would require more memorization—for example, short poems or important passages. The reason for this would be because they would often appear in entrance examinations.

In America, I am tested on what I thought about a certain poem or a certain passage.

The teachers in Japan are treated with a higher degree of respect than in the U.S. Each day, we would bow and greet our teachers before class or in the halls. In Japan I was thinking of becoming a teacher. Now, in the U.S., I do not think I want to become a teacher.

In American schools, I have learned to use my mind creatively. I feel that I am an individual here, with choices not only of what I wear to school, but what kind of courses I take. For instance, I am taking a business law class because I think it will help me to learn more about the law and conducting business.

Also in Winston Churchill High School, I have met more different kinds of people from other countries or different cultures.

Next year if I went back to Japan, I would need at least one and one-half years of school to be prepared to go to college. However, I am hoping to attend an American university and study business, because I think it is challenging and rewarding.

Thank you very much for this opportunity. I look forward to answering your questions.

The CHAIRMAN. Thank you very much. You are very good to come and appear here.

I understand that you enjoy the Winston Churchill School at the present time, do you not?

Mr. MURAKAMI. Yes, I do.

The CHAIRMAN. And you find that challenging.

Mr. MURAKAMI. Yes, I do.

The CHAIRMAN. I hear it is a first-rate school.

Can you elaborate a little bit on the attitudes, what you think are really the best in terms of what you have seen in your American experience, and maybe what is the weakest? Maybe we could start with that, and then I will ask you the same question with regards to the Japanese experience and how you, as a young person, come out.

Let us start with the American experience, first. What do you find?

Mr. MURAKAMI. Well, I think people who are really going for the top, people who want a good education, have the same attitude as anybody else would in the world. But I believe that some people do not really care what is going to become of them from now.

In Japan, I believe everybody has the same attitude. You have a lot more competition around you because you must succeed. And there is a lot more pressure put upon the student. Also, I believe that the Japanese parents, especially the mother, gets a lot more involved in the child's activities in school and out, which helps the child to understand what he or she must do.

The CHAIRMAN. Could you elaborate on that point, about the parents becoming involved—I know your father helps you a good deal, too. Could you tell us a little bit about some of the parental involvement in education in Japan?

Mr. MURAKAMI. When the student comes home, in most families the mother would quickly put him to work, such as his homework, or he would have to go to Juku, and the mother helps him with his homework so that he fully understands the course so he can pass the course. Whereas in America, I do not think there is as much parental involvement with the student.

The CHAIRMAN. This to some extent is true about your father, as well, is it not?

Mr. MURAKAMI. Yes, it is.

The CHAIRMAN. Did he involve himself in the math and science?

Mr. MURAKAMI. My mother would have helped me if she could, but since she is an American, she was not able to help me in courses such as social studies or Japanese. And for the first couple of months, or half-year or so, my father helped me every Sunday for quite a long period on all the courses so I could keep up and catch up with the other students in the school.

The CHAIRMAN. That is wise advice from another society, I think, in terms of involving the parents in the education.

If you were to go on to college or a university in Japan, having graduated from high school—and I am just talking about any high school to the extent that you know about it—would you have to take additional courses, or would you have to have, so to speak, a beefing-up to gain entrance into a Japanese university?

Mr. MURAKAMI. At this point, even if I graduated Winston Churchill, I believe I would need at least another year and a half to prepare to go to college. That would primarily be because of my lack of Japanese ability at the moment since I have not been attending Japanese school; and of course, the social studies, but especially in the math and the science, I think I would probably be behind.

The CHAIRMAN. Let me ask finally, what do you think is the best part of the Japanese educational system and the part you would most question?

Mr. MURAKAMI. I think that the best part is that there is only one course that they offer in the major courses such as science, social studies, English, Japanese and mathematics, which means that the students are all treated equal; they must pass the same course as any fellow student. Whereas in America, some people who cannot do as well as others would take an easier course. And I think that students all start from one, and if they all try as hard as they can, I think that they can all be just as good as one another. But if you have easier courses to offer, then the ones that do not want to work as hard are going to go down, and the ones who want to work harder are going to keep on going up.

The CHAIRMAN. Let me just ask two questions. Why is it that you would have wanted to be a teacher in Japan and not here?

Mr. MURAKAMI. First of all, in Japan, I have the English ability, pronunciation-wise, higher than most Japanese teachers. In Japan, everybody must take English, and I was often used as an example of how to read, for my pronunciation. The English teachers in Japan are not quite as good as I think they should be.

So one reason is that I could probably easily become an English teacher. Another reason is that they are highly respected in society. I think all the parents respect them; they get a lot of respect, and I think I would enjoy being a teacher.

The CHAIRMAN. Do you think that is important that the teacher have respect, from the students' point of view?

Mr. MURAKAMI. I think it is, because the students learn to respect their teachers and their elders, and I think that is one of the reasons for success in the Japanese educational system.

The CHAIRMAN. Senator Stafford?

Senator STAFFORD. Thank you, Mr. Chairman.

Shin, when you referred to the fact that everybody in Japan has to take mathematics and presumably, succeed, I am just asking this question because you also said that in this country you could take easier courses. We are not all exactly alike, and some people are better at mathematics than others, and others are better at studying the nation's literature or at beginning to lay a background for medicine or psychology.

I wonder if maybe the American system might be at least equally as good if it allows you to turn from mathematics to something that mentally, you are suited at doing much better than at mathematics. Could you comment on that?

Mr. MURAKAMI. Yes, I do think so. As I mentioned, I take a business law course because I am interested in that subject. And in that area, I think America really offers the student a choice of what he or she wants to do, and I think that is great.

But when asked why, maybe one of the reasons why the U.S. is lower, or not at as high right now in the world, I would have to answer that maybe that is one of the reasons, that you have easier alternatives to take.

Senator STAFFORD. Without prying into your personal life too much—and no further than you want us to—could I ask you what sort of grading system is used in Japan vis-a-vis this country and how you do in grades in both countries?

Mr. MURAKAMI. In Japan they go by 1, 2, 3, 4, 5—5 being an A, 4 being a B, and so on. I was able to barely get a 2 or a 3, which would be a C or a D, in most of my classes.

Senator STAFFORD. How do you do in this country?

Mr. MURAKAMI. I try to push myself and take the hard courses, so to say, and I get about a C or a B average.

Senator STAFFORD. Well, I certainly join the Chairman in thanking you for coming here today. I recall in the last Congress we had a Vietnamese student who was in this country's school system at the eleventh grade. And he said he was bored with some math courses he was taking here, and when we asked him why, he said it was because he had already taken those courses two years earlier in Vietnam.

So Japan may not be the only country that is forcing an intellectual development in mathematics and science, and quite strongly, at an early age.

Mr. MURAKAMI. Yes.

Senator STAFFORD. Thank you very much.

Thank you, Mr. Chairman.

The CHAIRMAN. Senator Harkin?

Senator HARKIN. Thank you, Mr. Chairman.

Shin, I think that is very interesting. I just want to ask you a couple of questions about the Jukus. Jukus are private tutoring are they not?

Mr. MURAKAMI. That is correct.

Senator HARKIN. Japanese students who go to Juku in the evening—that costs money, does it not?

Mr. MURAKAMI. Yes, that would.

Senator HARKIN. Not all Japanese students go to Juku, do they?

Mr. MURAKAMI. Not all.

Senator HARKIN. Those who come from families who can afford it go, don't they?

Mr. MURAKAMI. Yes, I would guess that would be the case.

Senator HARKIN. Would that be the case?

Mr. MURAKAMI. Right.

Senator HARKIN. The question I have is, if the Japanese educational system is so good, why is it necessary for students to have private tutoring in the evenings, and again, students that do tend to be those from higher income families. They have a leg up in the schools because of the private tutoring that they receive. Is that basically true?

Mr. MURAKAMI. Yes, it could be. All I know as a student is that without the Juku, I definitely would not be able to go to a good high school. Just with the educational system, if you worked hard, you could get into any school that you wanted to get into—if you worked harder than anybody else. That would mean even if you are not going to Juku, you would have to study that much more at home. A lot of kids have their parents help them, like I said, which would be something that would take the Juku's place.

I know a lot of kids, my friends, who have gotten into good schools without going to Juku. In my case, I had to be pushed by somebody because my father works and, like I said, my mother could not help me as much as my friends. And that is the reason I went to Juku.

I think, though, that 60 or 70 percent of students probably do go to Juku, and you learn a lot more material there, and you learn a lot of things that come out on the high school entrance examination. Getting into a good high school is sort of like a ticket to success in Japan. The better the high school, the better the college you get into, and the better the college, the name, in the country, you get into a better business.

Senator HARKIN. Could you just talk a little bit from your own background about the difference between the physical facilities, schools? What are the schools physically like in Japan, compared to the Potomac high school that you go to, Winston Churchill? How do they differ?

Mr. MURAKAMI. I do not see much of a difference. I think in America, you have a lot more playground area for different kinds of sports. That is probably because of the land situation. You do not have rugs and so on inside the school in America, which I had in my elementary school.

Senator HARKIN. I ask that because I lived in Japan for a year and a half, and I did visit quite a few schools, and it seemed to me that the physical facilities were much starker—I do not want to say less nice, but there was just a building, and there were rooms, and there were blackboards, and of course there were laboratories and things like that, too—but that not a lot of emphasis was put on the niceties and appearances and things like that.

Mr. MURAKAMI. No.

Senator HARKIN. I had a question about the grading, but you answered that.

I think that there is a lot we can learn from the Japanese educational system and a lot that we can adopt in terms of discipline and respect, and emphasis on certain items. But I think you really hit upon the key thing on why I am basically proud of the American system of education. It is universal. As you point out, it involves people from different races and cultures and puts them all together, teaches everyone, teaches them how to live together—plus, it teaches our kids how to think creatively. I think you really hit on it, and I appreciate it.

In my conversations with my Japanese friends, that is the one thing they always point out is that the Japanese are taught the mathematics, they are taught the sciences, but it is the creative part that they say that they are lacking, and that is what we do so well in this country. I think that is really the strongest part of our educational system.

Mr. MURAKAMI. One thing I would like to say about that is that although the Japanese do not stress creative writing or creativity, for some reason or another, the Japanese have a lot of creativeness—as you can see if you have seen Japanese paintings or drawings that the Japanese have drawn, or anything, even after they get into business—the Walkman, the Watchman. Where they come up with these ideas, I would not really know, but I think they are very creative. Maybe it is something they are born with. So that could be one reason the Japanese do not stress creativity; they learn by themselves, somehow or another.

Senator HARKIN. Thank you very much.

Mr. MURAKAMI. Thank you.

The CHAIRMAN. Shin, we were talking about tutorial schools. They have quite a tradition here in this country, too. Manter Hall used to be a great support school up at Harvard, particularly before the war, but it still exists rudimentarily. That was available to students both at Harvard and MIT—which, as you may have heard, are two of our good universities.

Now there are increasing numbers of schools for young people who are taking the SATs. I saw that in a personal way; my son took the test and then went back and took one of these courses, which was just done over Christmas-time for a period of about ten days, and had a significant increase—close to 100 points in the reading area, and about 40 points in math. I do not know whether that says something about him or something about the test. And now they are taking a prime for the law aptitude test, which they did not do when I was taking the law aptitude, and I think all law graduates are familiar with the bar review course that most of us were involved in, for the most part, before taking the bar exam in our own State.

So this has a tradition. It is perhaps not as elaborate or involved as it is in Japan, but it is something that exists here.

I want to thank you very, very much for your very helpful and very interesting testimony. We are grateful to you and wish you the best luck in whatever career you choose.

Mr. MURAKAMI. Thank you.

The CHAIRMAN. Thank you very much.

Our next panel includes Paul Barton, the Associate Director of the National Assessment of Educational Progress, who will speak to us about the report on "Literacy: Profiles of America's Young Adults"; and Lewis Branscomb, former Vice President of IBM, Director of Science, Technology and Public Policy Program at the John F. Kennedy School of Government, with a report on "A Nation Prepared: Teachers for the 21st Century" from the Carnegie Forum on Education and the Economy.

We are glad to have Mr. Branscomb back. He used to come and appear years ago when I used to be Chairman of the National Science Foundation and talk to us about Science and Education at the NSF. So he has been appearing before these committees for almost as many years as I have been on them.

Mr. Barton, we know you have been enormously helpful to all of us in this area.

We will ask Mr. Barton if you will be good enough to begin. I will be absent for about three minutes during the course of this presentation. I just want to mention that to the witnesses. I just got an unavoidable call, and I will ask Senator Harkin to preside while I am gone. But I will be right back.

Mr. Barton, please proceed.

STATEMENT OF PAUL E. BARTON, ASSOCIATE DIRECTOR, NATIONAL ASSESSMENT OF EDUCATIONAL PROGRESS, EDUCATIONAL TESTING SERVICE; AND DR. LEWIS BRANSCOMB, FORMER VICE PRESIDENT, IBM, AND DIRECTOR, SCIENCE, TECHNOLOGY AND PUBLIC POLICY PROGRAM, JOHN F. KENNEDY SCHOOL OF GOVERNMENT, HARVARD UNIVERSITY, CAMBRIDGE, MA

Mr. BARTON. Thank you, Mr. Chairman.

Mr. Chairman and members of the Committee, high proportions of young adults have quite limited literacy skills, although most

Handout #12

Name_____

1. Each subcommittee member should share the portions of testimony he or she marked which had to do with similarities and differences between Japanese and American education. Other members may agree or disagree, and should share those opinions. Not ALL members must agree on every point.

2. Members may also wish to discuss the following:

   a. As members of Congress seeking to review goals of American Education, do you feel that Mr. Murakami left certain questions unanswered? What more would you like to know concerning the two contrasting systems of education? Where might you get the answers you are looking for? You may wish to address these additional questions in your report and direct the reader's attention to suggested resources, if any.

   b. Did you feel that Mr. Murakami preferred one system over the other? Find statements he made to support your answers. Might his Japanese heritage have influenced his statements? Might an American with similar experiences have felt differently?

   c. Do you disagree with any of Mr. Murakami's testimony based on your own experience? Discuss your feelings with your subcommittee.

   d. Do you find yourself feeling that one system is preferable over the other? If so, in what ways? Do you feel that your opinions will be reflected in your report to your state? Should they be? Why or why not?

Handout #13

World Hunger: A Growing Crisis

The pain in the pit of your stomach spreads like a slow-moving cancer. As the days pass, every part of your body begins to ache, to cry out for help. But no help is there. Your body begins actually to eat itself in in a desperate search for energy. First, it dissolves its own fat cells. When these are gone, it dissolves its muscle cells until they, too, are gone and your legs and arms are little more than skin-covered bones.

Your neck is now so thin that it can barely hold your bony head. Your breath comes in short gasps, as if your lungs can't get enough air. Finally, your weakened heart simply stops beating…

That is what it is like to starve to death—a fate most Americans will probably never have to worry about. But according to a new report from the World Food Council, a branch of the United Nations, starvation and hunger now affect more people worldwide, than ever before. The UN defines hunger as a condition in which a poor diet deprives people "of the food they need to enjoy active healthy lives."

According to the UN report, the number of hungry people in the world grew by 15 million from 1970 to 1980, an increase of about 1.5 million a year. Between 1980 and 1985, however, the number of the world's hungry increased by nearly 8 million a year, reaching 512 million by last year—a number more than double the U.S. population.

Source: *Current Events*, Vol. 87, #13, December 18, 1987.

What happens when you fast

Each of us is an expert at eating. A few of us might even be described as "militant eaters" veteran faster Dick Gregory's mordant phrase for people who "attack" their food.

Not eating, on the other hand, is largely unknown and unfamiliar to many people in the United States.

Most of us living in rich countries eat more than we need to survive. The rhythm of our meals does not correspond to what our bodies

actually need, nor is this daily food intake needed to replace extended body reserves. In fact, most people can safely fast for 30 days without depriving themselves of body fuel needed to sustain life.

A healthy adult uses 1-1.2 calories per minute, 1,500 to 1,800 calories per day, just to maintain bodily functions. A typical active adult may require up to twice that number. An athlete, or someone who does hard physical work, may expend as many as 5,000-6000 calories in a day.

The weakness or headache sensation of hunger that you may experience during your fast is a temporary reaction to these shifts from one energy source to another.

It is useful to understand the difference between hunger and appetite. Hunger is a body need which has a physiological basis: the sensation of true hunger and its accompanying reaction—eating—are necessary to sustain human life.

Appetite is essentially a psychological impulse which motivates one to seek pleasure through the act of eating. It is usually appetite and not hunger which motivates us to eat three times a day.

The body is well adapted to going without food for short periods of time.

As the glucose in the blood is depleted, the body begins to draw on its stored glucose, or glycogen, from the liver to ensure an adequate supply to the brain. The other organs and tissues begin to use the relatively large quantity of calories stored as body fat for their own energy requirements.

What happens to your body when it is deprived of food, the source of those calories? After a meal, there is a four-to-five hour supply of glucose (a simple sugar) in the bloodstream to meet the body's energy needs. Glucose is the primary fuel of the central nervous system. Without it, the brain cannot survive for more than a few minutes.

Source: Oxfam America's *Organizer's Guide*

Handout #14

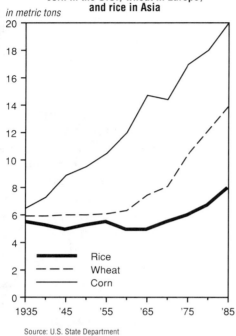

Rising Abundance
Yields, or production per acre of corn in the U.S., wheat in Europe, and rice in Asia

in metric tons

Source: U.S. State Department

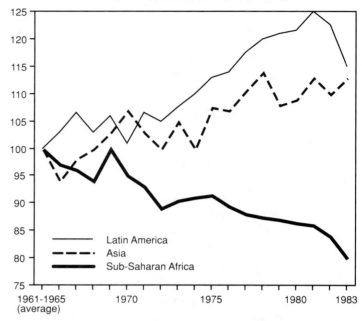

Food Production
Per person, compared to 1961-65 average

- Latin America
- Asia
- Sub-Saharan Africa

Source: The World Bank

Percentage of Population in 87 Developing Nations Receiving Not Enough Calories

	For an active working life %	Population in millions	To present stunted growth and serious health risks %	Population in millions
East Asia and the Pacific	7	20	14	40
South Asia	21	200	50	470
South of the Sahara in Africa	25	90	44	150
Middle East and North Africa	4	10	10	20
Latin America and the Caribbean	6	20	13	50
Total or Average	16	340	34	730

Source: The World Bank

Africa's Lost Children
Malnourished children aged 6 to 60 months

Mauritius	1,000	2%
Cape Verde	3,000	5%
Gabon	6,000	10%
Ivory Coast	230,000	15%
Cameroon	240,000	15%
Swaziland	20,000	17%
Botswana	30,000	18%
Lesotho	45,000	19%
Togo	100,000	20%
Sudan	710,000	22%
Kenya	820,000	23%
Liberia	90,000	23%
Nigeria	3,520,000	23%
Rwanda	210,000	23%
Guinea-Bissau	20,000	24%
Namibia	40,000	24%
Senegal	240,000	24%
Zaire	1,270,000	24%
Zimbabwe	350,000	24%
Burundi	190,000	25%
Congo	70,000	25%
Madagascar	400,000	25%
Tanzania	870,000	25%
Benin	180,000	26%
Niger	280,000	26%
Zambia	300,000	26%
Uganda	690,000	27%
Sierra Leone	180,000	28%
Somalia	250,000	28%
Mozambique	570,000	29%
Angola	400,000	30%
Mauritania	100,000	30%
Malawi	380,000	31%
Gambia	40,000	34%
Mali	440,000	34%
Chad	280,000	36%
Guinea	330,000	36%
Ethiopia	2,230,000	37%
Burkina Faso	520,000	40%

Source: Cornell University

Adapted from "A World In Need Of Help," *Scholastic Update*, December 15, 1986. Used by permission.

Handout #14

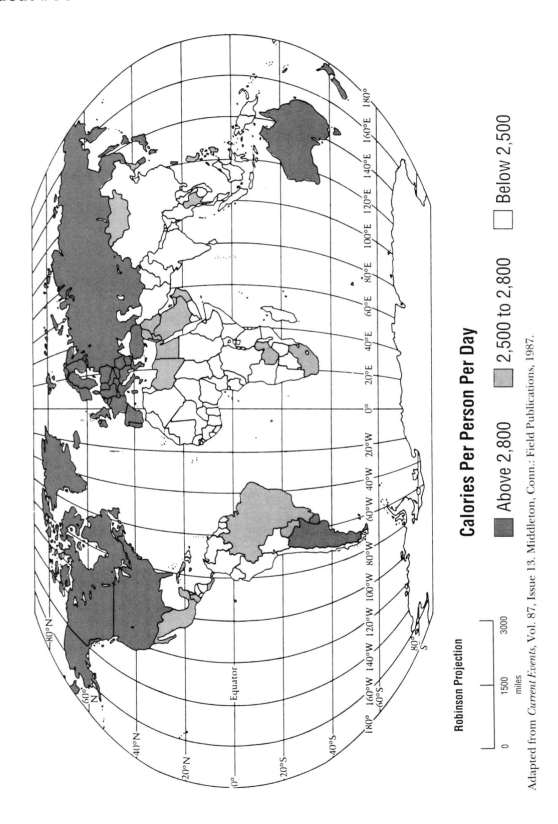

Calories Per Person Per Day

Above 2,800   2,500 to 2,800   Below 2,500

Robinson Projection

0   1500   3000
miles

Adapted from *Current Events*, Vol. 87, Issue 13. Middleton, Conn.: Field Publications, 1987.

Handout #15

Handout 16

Editorial

"Who should we help first?"

Recently, there has been a rash of "stop hunger" groups gaining popularity and support in the United States. It seems that a person cannot turn on the television without receiving a message from some celebrity to send money abroad to help children and families in distant parts of the world. What about the problems in our own country? There are several thousand Americans classified as homeless—surely many of these are hungry. If one U.S. child is starving, that is one too many. The hunger problem plagues our country as well as those far away. Must we help the *outside* first? Perhaps we should concentrate our efforts in our own backyard.

Handout #17

Name_____

Students publish two newspapers at Morgan High School. One, called *X-It*, is published by a group of very bright honor students without authorization from school officials. This newspaper has a reputation for its open criticism of school policy, personnel, certain members of the student body, and whoever and whatever it wishes to malign. Although *X-It* devotes most of its pages to articles about current trends in music, fashion, and art, as well as a great deal of students' creative writing of a radical nature, the front page usually covers "current events" having to do with school activities and occurrences. This radical, anti-establishment tabloid is published off-campus, but school officials allow its distribution during school hours and on the school grounds.

The second is called *The Morgan Times*. It is the "official" newspaper for the school, honor students also make up its staff, two English teachers serve as advisors, and the administration of the school has final authority over it. This paper is usually pro-establishment and supports a somewhat conservative view of school life.

Read the following two excerpts from front-page articles that appeared in the two newspapers on the same day. In groups of three to four, complete the two activities that follow the articles. Be sure you note those points you feel are helpful to your understanding of bias news reporting.

1. "...As the four administrators attempted to explain the obvious need for a "closed campus" policy for the protection of our students, unruly members of the audience lashed out at them, screaming derision and obscenities. Embarrassing the more responsible students around them, a few even threw objects at the podium, leaving what was intended to be a rally for positive change in total chaos..."

2. "...The principal, vice principal, and two guidance counselors appeared yesterday in a special assembly of the student body to address the "closed campus" issue. As reported last week, based upon only three minor incidents involving off-campus alcohol and drug consumption during lunch-break, administrators arbitrarily elected to prohibit students from leaving school grounds during lunch and between classes. Administrators billed yesterday's assembly as a "rally" to gain student support for their decision. The students, however, responded with shouts and other reactions as administrators spoke, clearly voicing their disgust with this example of encroaching dictatorial rule here at Morgan High..."

Activity 1

Discuss the following with your group: News articles are intended to report current events objectively—without bias or opinion. Does either of of the articles contain bias? Do both? See if your group can write a definition of "bias." Look at a copy of the U.S.

Constitution (there should be one in most U.S. History textbooks). What does bias have to do with the First Amendment to our Constitution?

Activity 2

As a group, circle words and phrases in the articles that imply the reporter was biased. (Be careful! Sometimes bias is quite subtle). Do all members of your group readily agree on what comprises bias? Now compare your decisions with those of the other groups. Is there agreement? Can all groups come up with an agreeable definition? What can your class now say about bias? Does the fact that it is hard to define and even harder to identify have implications for how we read and listen to news?

Activity 3

On your own, try this: Using the information from both articles, write an objective (unbiased) report of the Morgan High incident.

Handout #18a

Name_____

The following is a first person, true-life account of an incident that occurred in the 1970s. The writer is a citizen of Rombique serving as a missionary in a foreign country we shall call Larovina.

We shall withhold the true identity of both countries. During the time of the missionary's service, the Larovonia government accused him of writing an article for a Rombican publication that criticized the government of Larovina, the country in which he was serving. Following the accusation, he was arrested and imprisoned. His description of the treatment he received in prison follows. Such treatment went on for three weeks, after which he was released and deported.

"They began asking where I was taking my car and what I was doing with my friend Alanir. They weren't interested in the answers; they asked the questions and started hitting me, before I had a chance to answer. I was subjected to about twenty (20) minutes of this kind of questioning, which was designed to disorient and thoroughly intimidate me. I was kicked in the groin three times in succession, until I was laid out altogether, and then I was forced to get up again for more questions and beatings.

"Then all of a sudden there was this complete silence and everybody left except one guy. I heard him filling a bucket with water which he poured on my legs and and on the floor around me. Then he came back with electrodes fastening one to the second toe of my right foot and the other fastened with a spring-clip to the nipple of my right breast, cutting right into the flesh. I knew what I was in for because electric shock is their standard torture technique. He went back and sat down at what must have been a table and began asking the same questions—only this time with each question would come an electric shock.

"The current would increase in voltage to the point of producing muscular convulsions and I would be thrown to the floor. Then he would turn the current off, and if I didn't get up rapidly enough, even with my hands handcuffed behind my back on the wet floor with no clothes on, he would turn on the current with light doses, like a cattle prod. As soon as I would get on my feet again, it would be the same thing: more questions, turning on the shock, increasing the voltage until I would be thrown to the floor again.

"I think the first session was about an hour and a half, counting the beatings and the shocks. By that time I was really just sort of in limbo, which is I think a physiological and psychological defense mechanism. You get to the point where it is not real. You are really not even there anymore; you are just kind of hanging on. It was all sort of a big blur. And when they became aware of that, they stopped, because they don't want you to get to that position; you aren't hurting enough." (from Cannon, Clark, and Smuga. *The Contemporary World*. Edinburgh: Oliver and Boyd, 1987)

Handout 18b

Universal Declaration of Human Rights

One of the first major achievements of the United Nations was the adoption by the General Assembly, on 10 December 1948, of the Universal Declaration of Human Rights. The Assembly proclaimed the Declaration as "a common standard of achievement for all peoples and nations," and it called upon Member States and all peoples to promote and secure the effective recognition and observance of the rights and freedoms set forth in the Declaration.

In 1950, the General Assembly decided that 10 December of each year should be observed as Human Rights Day all over the world.

Articles 1 and 2 of the Declaration state that "all human beings are born free and equal in dignity and rights" and are entitled to all the rights and freedoms set forth in the Declaration, "without distinction of any kind, such as race, colour, sex, language, national or social origin, property, birth or other status."

Articles 3 to 21 of the Declaration set forth the civil and political rights to which all human beings are entitled, including:

- the right to life, liberty and security of person;
- freedom from slavery and servitude;
- freedom from torture or cruel, inhuman or degrading treatment or punishment;
- the right to recognition as a person before the law; equal protection of the law; the right to an effective judicial remedy; freedom from arbitrary arrest, detention, or exile; the right to a fair trial and public hearing by an independent and impartial tribunal; the right to be presumed innocent until proven guilty;
- freedom from arbitrary interference with privacy, family, home, or correspondence;
- freedom of movement; the right to asylum; the right to nationality;
- the right to marry and to found a family: the right to own property;
- freedom of thought, conscience and religion; freedom of opinion and expression;
- the right of association and assembly;
- the right to take part in government and the equal access to public service.

Articles 22 to 27 of the Declaration set forth the economic, social and cultural rights to which all human beings are entitled, including:

- the right to social security;
- the right to work; the right to rest and leisure;
- the right to a standard of living adequate for health and well-being:
- the right to education;
- the right to participate in the cultural life of the community.

The concluding articles—28 to 30—recognize that everyone is entitled to a social and international order in which these rights and freedoms may be fully realized, and they stress the duties and responsibilities which the individual owes to the community.

Handout #19

The tropical rain forests of the world grow between the tropics of Cancer and Capricorn, where the climate and the rainfall is heavy and regular. Thirty-seven countries contain rainforests, the three largest being Brazil, Zaire, and Indonesia. Rain forests contain approximately half of all the species of plants and animals on earth—a veritable ark of five million species. These forests have the highest diversity, as well as a tremendous density, of living things on earth. A visitor to a rain forest experiences a verdant, dark, wet world of incredibly rich complexity. A cacophony of sound heralds the life within: insects chirp, frogs croak, birds sing, and monkeys screech.

From *Human Society News*, 32, 4, Fall 1987

Handout #20

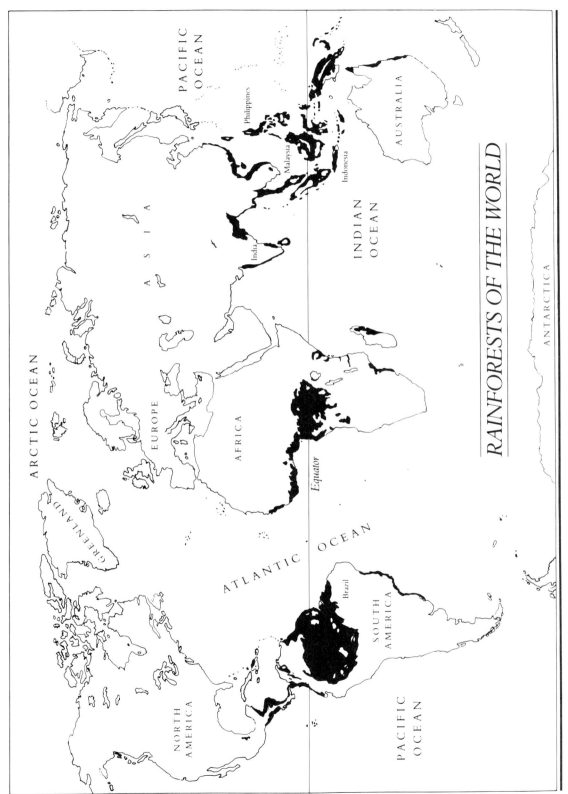

RAINFORESTS OF THE WORLD

Handout #21

Tropical forests form a green band around the Equator, extending roughly 10 degrees North and South. This means that they account for only a small portion, about 8 percent, of the Earth's land surface. Yet they comprise almost half of all growing wood on the face of the planet, and harbor at least two-fifths of Earth's plant and animal species, a genetic resource of increasing importance to humanity through agriculture, medicine and industry. They also comprise the most complex and diverse ecosystems on Earth, which fulfill regulatory and productive functions that are essential to humans and to their natural environment.

from *World Eagle* 11, 5, January, 1988

The wildlife and plantlife diversity of the Emerald Forest (as the Amazon rain forest is often called) is unmatched by any other region in the world. It has half of the world's known bird species, as well as 2,000 species of fish and another 4,000 species of butterfly.

from *Fast Times* 6, 2, February, 1989

The U.S. National Academy of Sciences estimates that a typical four-square-mile patch of rain forest contains up to 1,500 species of flowering plant, 700 tree species, 125 mammal species, 400 bird species, 100 reptile species, 60 amphibian species, and thousands of species of butterflies, ants, bees, and other insects.

from *Humane Society News* 32, 4, Fall, 1981

Handout #22

Tropical forests provide us with many useful and renewable products, including natural oils and resins, gums, latexes, tannins, steroids, waxes, edible nuts and oils, bamboo and spices. Many important pharmaceuticals are derived from rain forest plants and animals, including curare (used in modern surgery and to treat multiple sclerosis) and the Madagascar periwinkle (used to treat Hodgkin's Disease and lymphocytic leukemia successfully). Several anesthetics, contraceptives, anti-tumor agents, and heart medicines are derived from tropical forest plants. Forest tribal peoples know of countless other plants with great medicinal benefits, but when the forests are gone, their way of life and knowledge will disappear, along with thousands of potentially useful plant species.

from *Humane Society News* 32, 4, Fall, 1987

Coffee, papaya, bananas, brazilian nuts for example, come from the Amazon region. The rubber from its trees is used to make surgical gloves, airplane tires, and other important products, whereas about 25 percent of the prescription drugs we use contain at least one ingredient from the Amazon region. This includes curare, used by the Peruvian Indians to make poison arrows, and now being used in heart surgery to relax the heart muscle. Even the toothpaste you use in the morning has Amazon ingredients.

from *Fast Times* 6, 2, February, 1989

Handout #23

Handout #24

Yellow

Yellow never wants help,
But steps right out on its own,
Throwing bright light everywhere.

Yellow dashes through flower gardens,
Splashes on fried eggs,
Drips on traffic lights,
And wraps itself around bananas.

Yellow reaches out from the sun,
And never gives up.
Yellow is BOLD.

Brown

Brown is a brownie,
And brown is my dog.
Brown is a chocolate shake.
Boxes are brown.
Root beer is brown.
Foxes are brown, too.
Brown is a winter day.
Brown is a frown.
Brown is gingerbread baking.
Homework is brown.

Having to get up and go to school in the
    morning,
Getting into fights with your friend
Eating something you don't like—
All these are brown.

Being punished is brown.
Brown is getting warm on a cold day,
Or having your foot fall asleep.

Green

Green is the quiet of
    a secret garden
The smell of mint,
A cricket's chirp,
Pickles,
And a leprechaun.

Green is the mountains
    and algae-filled ponds,
Happiness and mold.
It's the feeling you
    get when you have
        the flu.

Green is sour.
It's broccoli and
    lizards, celery
and loneliness.

Cold is green,
And frostbite.
Green is lime
And crunchy salads.

Handout #25

_____(Title)

A Rain Forest is _____ and _____

(from list 1) and _____ (from list 4). A Rain Forest is the

taste of _____ (from list 6). _____

and _____ smell like a Rain Forest (list 3).

_____ makes me feel like a Rain Forest (list 5). A Rain

Forest is the sound of _____ and

_____(list 2). A Rain Forest is _____,

and _____ (list 8). _____ is a

Rain Forest (list 7). _____ is also a Rain Forest (list 7).

A Rain Forest is _____ (any list).

Handout #26

Margaret Frances Ashby Washington, 66, former Knoxville school teacher, dies

Margaret Frances Ashby Washington, a civic leader in the YWCA, the Girl Scouts, and the African Methodist Episcopal Church, died yesterday at a nursing home in Prince George's County, Md., after a lingering illness.

Mrs. Washington, who lived in Knoxville from 1960 to 1970, was a former president of the AME Women of Knoxville and served as president of the Greater Tennessee Women's Club headquartered in Knoxville.

Mrs. Washington also lived in Kingsport for several years. While there she served on the school board, and was president of several organizations including the Women's Literary Group, the NAACP, and the AME Church-women of the St. Paul African Methodist Episcopal Church of Kingsport.

She was a graduate of Spelman College in Atlanta, Georgia, and received her master's degree from Columbia University.

Survivors include her husband, William Herbert Washington of Knoxville, a son, William Herbert Washington, Jr., of St. Louis, Missouri, and a daughter, Angela Frances Washington Hood of Santa Cruz, California, and three grandchildren.

A memorial service will be at 1 p.m. Sunday at the Trinity African Methodist Episcopal Church in Knoxville, Tenn. Contributions may be made to the American Cancer Society.

Richard Boone, former hardware store owner, descendent of famous pioneer, dies

BLOWING ROCK—Richard Everett Boone, a former hardware store owner and descendant of the American pioneer, Daniel Boone, who settled the Appalachian area, died Sunday at Watauga General Hospital of kidney failure. He was 98.

Boone was the son of the late Jonathan Russell and Katherine Anne Younce and was the last surviving child of 12.

Boone, of 412 Somerset Drive, was owner of Rick's Hardware in Boone for 27 years. Boone operated the store for 40 years before retiring.

Boone had been an active member of the Boone Fisherman's club and was one of the oldest members of the group.

He also served in the army during World War I where he served as cook.

Boone was a member of St. John Lutheran Church in Boone.

Survivors include one son, William Boone of Blowing Rock, four daughters; Jane Marsh of Boone, Rosemary Jackson of Asheville, Wilma Jenkins of Hickory, and Julia Harper of Blowing Rock, ten grandchildren, and six great-grandchildren.

Services will be at 11 a.m. Wednesday at St. John Lutheran Church. burial will be in Rolling Hills Memorial Gardens, Boone, N.C. Visitation will be from 6 to 9 p.m. today.

Former Charlotteville police captain dies

MORGANTOWN—Marshall J. Crook, a former Charlotteville County police captain died Monday at his home. Crook, of Lakeside Drive, was 64.

He was a Morgantown police officer for 20 years and became captain of the Charlotteville County police force in 1960.

Crook was wounded in the line of duty and received recognition from the governor as Outstanding Office of the Year in 1954.

He was a member of the Knights of Columbus and served as Little League Baseball umpire.

Survivors include his wife, Penny Crook; three sons, John Crook of Campbell, Timothy Crook of Tempe, Ariz., and Marshall Jr., of Morgantown; a daughter, Melinda Crook Burroughs of Clearwater, Fla.; two sisters, and four grandchildren.

Services will be at 1 p.m. Thursday at Our Lady of Grace Catholic Church. Visitation will be after 2 p.m. today at Morgantown Funeral Home.

DIED. Norma Feinman, 88, painter and sculptor who influenced American abstract painting in the 1930s and 1940s and founded the New York Women's School of Painting in Albany in the early 1960s. A self-taught painter, Feinman briefly taught painting at the Sommerville School for girls in up-state New York before embarking on her well-known career in abstract art. Feinman's simple style began catching the public's eye in 1935 with her first showing in New York City. Her collection of more than 50 abstract paintings and sculptures including favorites such as *The Awakening*, *Green Meadows*, and the *Girl's School* have been favorites with viewers across the country. Ms. Feinman is survived by her husband, playwright Leonard Feinman. She was a member of the Congregation Beit Simchat Torah in Albany.

DIED. Dr. Pedro Cavallo, 76, former research director of the National Council of Immunology and Virology and allergist who earned international acclaim for his discoveries on the environmental causes of allergies, immunological deficiencies, and viral infections. Under his direction the council sponsored hundreds of studies linking environmental illness and airtight buildings in the United States.

Handout #27

Each of you will be remembered for one vital solution you gave to the world; a solution that changed many lives and perhaps the course of history. Your obituary might include the following items:

1. Name
2. Age of death
3. Cause of death
4. Time and place of death
5. Family names—wife, husband, or other companion? children? relatives?
6. Education and career—degrees? honors?
7. Greatest achievement—solution of a world problem
   a. What was the problem?
   b. How did you solve it?
   c. How has the solution affected the world?
8. A brief headline that would appear in the paper along with the obituary.

APPENDICES

Appendix A

Economic, Educational, and Cultural Indexes of 16 Nations

Nation	Income[1]	Growth[2]	Unemployment[3]	Nobels[4]	College[5]	Tests[6]	Work Hours[7]	Divorce[8]	TV[9]
Switzerland	17,430	1.5	0.4	21.6	17	.	44.1	31	31.4
Sweden	14,870	1.3	3.1	32.4	37	22	35.6	53	38.1
Germany	13,450	1.6	6.1	9.5	26	24	40.7	9	33.7
U.S.A.	12,820	1.6	9.5	6.9	55	22	34.8	50	62.4
France	12,190	2.0	8.0	0.7	25	.	39.8	22	35.4
Canada	11,400	1.0	10.9	1.3	36	.	38.2	32	47.1
Australia	11,080	2.4	7.1	2.7	26	25	35.0	44	37.8
Japan	10,080	4.4	2.4	0.3	30	31	40.2	18	53.9
Britain	9,110	0.5	12.5	13.9	20	21	43.0	36	40.4
Italy	6,960	2.2	8.9	1.9	27	19	38.8	4	38.6
Spain	5,640	0.9	15.9	0.3	22	.	43.3	0	25.2
Singapore	5,240	9.6	6.7	0.1	8	.	48.8	1	16.6
Israel	5,160	3.6	5.1	2.5	26	.	35.4	14	15.0
Mexico	2,250	6.6	4.2	0.1	15	.	45.0	5	10.4
Brazil	2,220	3.9	6.9	0.0	3	.	48.0	7	12.2
Hungary	2,100	2.5	1.0	2.7	13	29	40.0	32	25.8

[1]Income: Gross domestic product (GDP) per capita, 1981
[2]Growth: GDP average annual growth rate percent, 1977-1982
[3]Unemployment: Unemployed percent of labor force, 1982
[4]Nobels: Number of prizes per 10 million population, 1901-1982
[5]College: Percent of 20- to 24-year-olds enrolled in higher education, 1979
[6]Tests: Science test scores of 14-year-olds, 1970-1971
[7]Work Hours: Average hours worked per week (nonagricultural), 1982
[8]Divorce: Percent of marriages ending in divorce, 1979
[9]TV: Number of television sets per 100 population, 1980

Note: Only 9 of the 16 countries participated in the 1970-1971 science survey of the International Association for the Evaluation of Educational Achievement.

Sources: *Economist*, December 24, 1983; Walberg 1983

Source: Alan C. Purves, ed. *International Comparison and Educational Reform.* Reprinted with permission of the Association for Supervision and Curriculum Development. Copyright © 1989 by the Association for Supervision and Curriculum Development. All rights reserved.

Appendix B

Hours Per Year

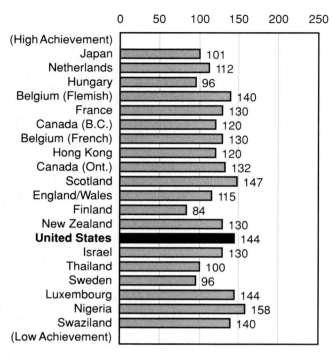

Country	Hours Per Year
(High Achievement)	
Japan	101
Netherlands	112
Hungary	96
Belgium (Flemish)	140
France	130
Canada (B.C.)	120
Belgium (French)	130
Hong Kong	120
Canada (Ont.)	132
Scotland	147
England/Wales	115
Finland	84
New Zealand	130
United States	144
Israel	130
Thailand	100
Sweden	96
Luxembourg	144
Nigeria	158
Swaziland	140
(Low Achievement)	

Days Per School Year

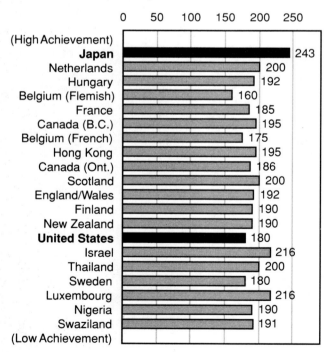

Country	Days Per School Year
(High Achievement)	
Japan	243
Netherlands	200
Hungary	192
Belgium (Flemish)	160
France	185
Canada (B.C.)	195
Belgium (French)	175
Hong Kong	195
Canada (Ont.)	186
Scotland	200
England/Wales	192
Finland	190
New Zealand	190
United States	180
Israel	216
Thailand	200
Sweden	180
Luxembourg	216
Nigeria	190
Swaziland	191
(Low Achievement)	

The length of the school year appears to show why Japan led in mathematics achievement at the Population A level. Countries are arranged in order of average score from high to low on the international test. The lack of a systematic relationship between length of school year in days and achievement can be inferred from the absence of an orderly pattern of decreasing lengths of school years from top to bottom.

Yearly hours of mathematics instruction at Population A provide a pattern that differs from the length of the school year. For example, Japan has the longest school year, but has one of the least amounts of school time devoted to mathematics. (Many Japanese students spend a considerable amount of time studying mathematics outside of regular school hours, however.) In the United States, the school year is relatively short, but a relatively large amount of that time is allocated to mathematics.

Deceptive Explanation Number One: Time for Mathematics Instruction

One popular candidate for explaining low achievement is the lack of sufficient time allocated for instruction—students learn primarily what they are taught, teaching takes time, and additional time devoted to instruction can reasonably be expected to result in gains in achievement.

Yet data from the Study indicate that the relationship between instructional time and achievement is neither simple nor linear. As the graph of our data indicates (see *Yearly hour of mathematical instruction*) some countries with *high* average achievement on the international test have a relatively *small* amount of time per year allocated to mathematics instruction (compare, for example, the U.S. and Japan). The data in the graph are for Population A, but similar findings were obtained for Population B.

Source: McKnight et al. *The Underachieving Curriculum: Assessing U.S. School Mathematics from an International Perspective.* Champaign, Ill.: Stipes Publishing Co., 1987.

Appendix C

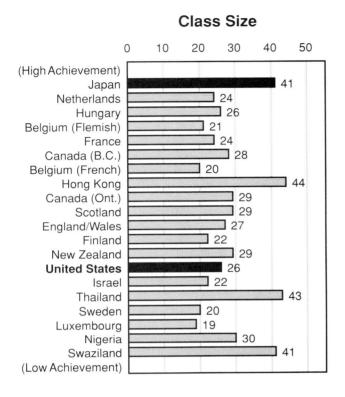

Class Size

(High Achievement)	
Japan	41
Netherlands	24
Hungary	26
Belgium (Flemish)	21
France	24
Canada (B.C.)	28
Belgium (French)	20
Hong Kong	44
Canada (Ont.)	29
Scotland	29
England/Wales	27
Finland	22
New Zealand	29
United States	26
Israel	22
Thailand	43
Sweden	20
Luxembourg	19
Nigeria	30
Swaziland	41
(Low Achievement)	

Class size is a deceptive explanation of level of achievement, as can be seen from this presentation of average class sizes (with countries arranged in order by achievement) for Population A. The four countries with largest classes are distributed throughout the ordered list of twenty countries, as are the four countries with the smallest class sizes.

Source: McKnight, et al. *The Underachieving Curriculum: Assessing U.S. School Mathematics from an International Perspective.* Champaign, Ill.: Stipes Publishing Company, 1987.

Appendix D

Table 288.—Public expenditures for education as a percentage of gross national product: Selected countries, 1960 to 1984

Country	1960	1970	1975	1979	1980	1981	1982	1983	1984
1	2	3	4	5	6	7	8	9	10
Australia	2.9	4.2	6.2	5.9	5.9	¹5.9	6.2	—	—
Canada	²4.6	8.9	7.8	7.7	7.7	7.8	¹8.3	¹7.7	—
Chile	²2.7	5.1	4.1	3.8	4.6	5.4	5.8	5.0	7.4
France	⁴2.4	4.9	¹5.2	—	5.1	¹5.6	5.8	—	4.8
Germany, Federal Republic of	—	¹3.5	5.1	4.6	4.7	4.7	4.6	4.5	—
Hungary⁹	4.4	4.4	4.1	4.1	4.7	5.1	5.0	5.8	5.4
Italy	⁶3.6	4.0	4.5	5.0	—	—	—	5.7	—
Japan	4.1	3.9	5.5	5.8	5.9	¹5.9	5.7	—	—
Mexico	²,³1.3	2.4	3.8	4.0	3.0	4.4	¹4.3	¹2.8	—
Netherlands	⁷4.9	7.3	8.2	8.1	7.9	7.9	7.7	—	—
Nigeria	⁴,⁹2.2	—	⁵4.3	3.9	—	—	¹2.1	¹2.2	—
Norway	4.2	6.0	7.1	—	¹7.2	6.9	7.0	7.0	—
Sweden	⁴4.6	7.7	7.1	9.1	9.1	9.2	9.0	¹8.4	8.0
Thailand	⁶,⁹2.5	3.5	3.6	3.2	3.3	3.7	3.9	3.9	—
United Kingdom	²4.3	5.3	6.7	5.4	¹5.7	¹5.5	¹5.4	5.3	—
United States	4.0	5.9	6.6	5.7	5.8	5.4	5.6	¹5.6	5.5
U.S.S.R.⁹	5.9	6.8	7.6	7.3	¹7.1	6.9	6.7	6.6	—
Yugoslavia	¹⁰2.5	4.9	5.4	5.4	¹5.1	4.5	¹4.4	3.9	—

¹Data revised from previously published figure.
²Data for 1961.
³Expenditures by the Ministry of Education only.
⁴As percentage of gross domestic product at market prices.
⁵As a percentage of net material product.
⁶Data for 1969.
⁷Includes private expenditures relating to private education.
⁸Data for 1976.

⁹Central or federal government only; not including foreign aid.
¹⁰As a percentage of gross material product.
—Data not available.

SOURCE: United Nations Educational, Scientific, and Cultural Organization, Paris, *Statistical Yearbook*; and U.S. Department of Commerce, Bureau of the Census, Governmental Finances, various years. (This table was prepared October 1987.)

Table 289.—Average percent of items answered correctly on an international mathematics test of 8th grade students: Selected countries, 1981-82

Country or province	Mean percent correct, all items¹	Arithmetic	Algebra	Geometry	Measurement	Statistics
1	2	3	4	5	6	7
Average	**47.4**	**50.5**	**43.1**	**41.4**	**50.8**	**54.7**
Belgium						
Flemish	53.2	58.0	52.9	42.5	58.2	58.2
French	51.4	57.0	49.1	42.8	56.8	52.0
Canada						
British Columbia	51.6	58.0	47.9	42.3	51.9	61.3
Ontario	49.0	54.5	42.0	43.2	50.8	57.0
England and Wales	47.2	48.2	40.1	44.8	48.6	60.2
Finland	46.8	45.5	43.6	43.2	51.3	57.6
France	52.5	57.7	56.0	38.0	59.5	57.4
Hong Kong²	49.4	55.1	43.2	42.5	52.6	55.9
Hungary	56.0	56.8	50.4	53.4	62.1	60.4
Israel	45.0	49.9	44.0	35.9	46.4	51.9
Japan²	62.1	60.3	60.3	57.6	68.6	70.9
Luxembourg	37.5	45.4	31.2	25.3	50.1	37.3
Netherlands	57.1	59.3	51.3	52.0	61.9	65.9
New Zealand	45.5	45.6	39.4	44.8	45.1	57.3
Nigeria	33.6	40.8	32.4	26.2	30.7	37.0
Scotland	48.4	50.2	42.9	45.5	48.4	59.3
Swaziland	31.5	32.3	25.1	31.1	35.2	36.0
Sweden	41.8	40.6	32.3	39.4	48.7	56.3
Thailand	42.2	43.1	37.7	39.3	48.3	45.3
United States	45.3	51.4	42.1	37.8	40.8	57.7

¹Weighted average determined by the number of items in each test component.
²Students in Japan and Hong Kong were attending the seventh grade.

SOURCE: U.S. Department of Education, Center for Education Statistics, contractor report,

Perceptions of the Intended and Implemented Curriculums by Ian Livingston. This table was based on the "Second International Mathematics Study" conducted by the International Association for the Evaluation of Educational Achievement. (This table was prepared October 1986.)

Appendix E

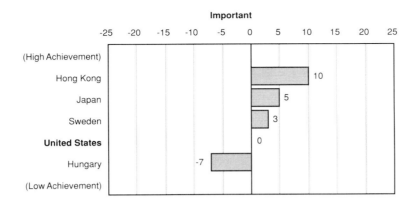

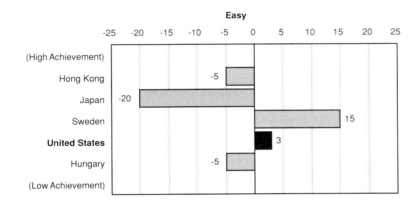

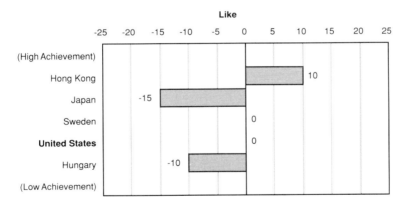

Activities in the last year of secondary school (Population B) mathematics classroom were also rated as to importance, ease, and whether they were liked. These activities included checking answers to problems, memorizing rules and formulae and proving theorems. As the above data indicate, the students in Hong Kong found these activities rather important, as did the Japanese. The Swedish students reported them to be easy. The Japanese found these activities hard and did not like them. Again, the U.S. students were, comparatively, somewhat "middle of the road" in their attitudes toward these activities.

Source: McKnight, et al. *The Underachieving Curriculum: Assessing U.S. School Mathematics from an International Perspective.* Champaign, Ill.: Stipes Publishing Company, 1987.

Appendix F

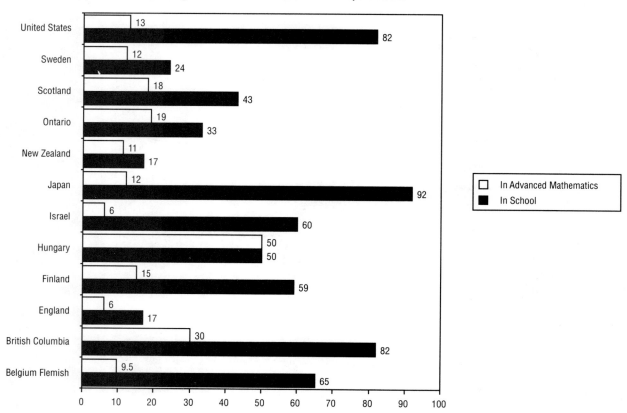

Participation in Schooling and Advanced Mathematics Population B

Country	In Advanced Mathematics	In School
United States	13	82
Sweden	12	24
Scotland	18	43
Ontario	19	33
New Zealand	11	17
Japan	12	92
Israel	6	60
Hungary	50	50
Finland	15	59
England	6	17
British Columbia	30	82
Belgium Flemish	9.5	65

Legend: ☐ In Advanced Mathematics ■ In School

The figures above represent the percentages of the cohort that are still in school and that which is taking advanced mathematics courses. The average age, number of years of schooling, and definition of advanced mathematics vary among educational systems. Students in Ontario are about one year older and are enrolled in grade 13, for instance. Although in most systems calculus is the standard content, that differs as well. In the United States, for example, only about 2 percent of the cohort is enrolled in a calculus course; less than one-half of them are enrolled in advanced placement calculus.

Source: Alan C. Purves, ed. *International Comparison and Educational Reform.* Reprinted with permission of the Association for Supervision and Curriculum Development. Copyright © 1989 by the Association for Supervision and Curriculum Development. All rights reserved.

Appendix G

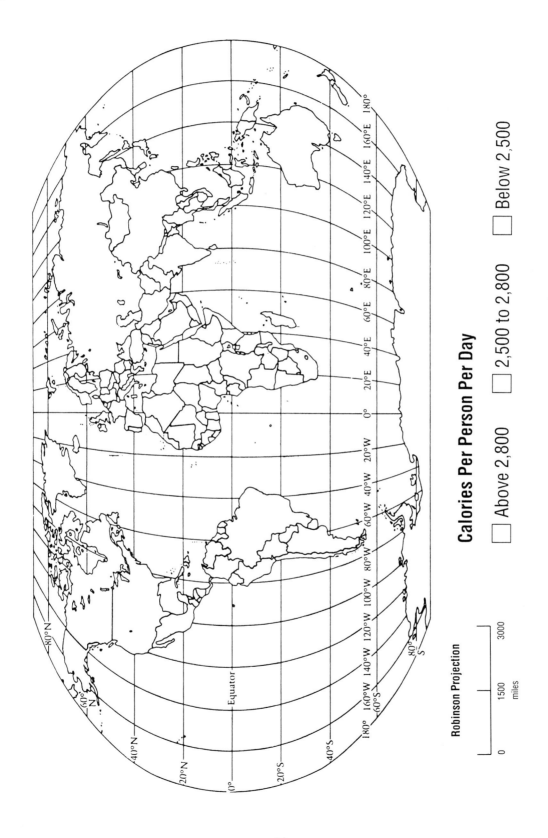

Calories Per Person Per Day

☐ Above 2,800   ☐ 2,500 to 2,800   ☐ Below 2,500

Robinson Projection

0   1500   3000
miles